YORK NOTES

›n and
Derbyshire Book› ... e r

Homer
The Iliad

(Translated by E.V. Rieu)

Note by Robin Sowerby

Longman York Press

Robin Sowerby is hereby identified as author of this work in accordance with Section 77 of the Copyright, Designs and Patents Act 1988

York Press
322 Old Brompton Road, London SW5 9JH

PEARSON EDUCATION LIMITED
Edinburgh Gate, Harlow,
Essex CM20 2JE, United Kingdom
Associated companies, branches and representatives throughout the world

© Librairie du Liban *Publishers* and Pearson Education Limited 2001

All rights reserved. No part of this publication may be reproduced, stored in a retrieval system, or transmitted in any form or by any means, electronic, mechanical, photocopying, recording, or otherwise, without either the prior written permission of the Publishers or a licence permitting restricted copying in the United Kingdom issued by the Copyright Licensing Agency Ltd, 90 Tottenham Court Road, London W1T 4LP.

First published 2001
15 14 13 12 11 10 9 8

ISBN: 978-0-582-43152-2

Designed by Vicki Pacey
Phototypeset by Gem Graphics, Trenance, Mawgan Porth, Cornwall
Colour reproduction and film output by Spectrum Colour
Printed in China (EPC/08)

Contents

Part one

Introduction

How to study an epic narrative poem (in prose translation)

Studying a long narrative poem on your own requires self-discipline and a carefully thought-out work plan in order to be effective.

- You will need to read the work more than once. Start by reading it quickly for pleasure, then read it slowly and thoroughly.
- On your second reading make detailed notes on the plot, characters and themes. Further readings will generate new ideas.
- Make sure you understand all the mythological references. Look names up in a dictionary if necessary.
- Remember that, though you are reading it in modern prose, the work is from a different culture and time. Make an imaginative effort to read it on its own terms, noting how it differs from modern stories set in the modern world.
- **Epic** poems feature epic heroes. What are the characteristics of heroic behaviour in this work and how do they differ from those exhibited by other heroic figures?
- Think about the way in which the narrative unfolds: the time-scheme and the different settings may be a key to its structure and organisation.
- Are words, images or motifs repeated so as to give the work a pattern? Do such patterns help you to understand the work's themes?
- It is difficult when commenting on a work in translation to make precise points about its style. But think of its style in broad terms, noting such features as the recurring **epithets**, the extended **similes**, the set speeches, the intervention of the divine. Compare with another translation if you can.
- Does the work present a moral and just world?
- Cite exact sources for all quotations. Wherever possible find your own examples from the work to back up your own opinions.
- Always express your ideas in your own words.

This York Note offers an introduction to the *Iliad* and cannot substitute for close reading of the text and the study of secondary sources.

The *Iliad*, together with the *Odyssey*, stands at the head of the Western tradition. In its great vision of life, affirming and celebrating the human spirit, and in the way it represents that vision, it embodies characteristically Greek values that underpin subsequent Greek culture and have been deeply influential ever since. It is the first great heroic poem not only in time but in its vision and themes. Few poems have so celebrated the vibrancy of life in the physical world. For the Homeric heroes, Greek and Trojan, aspire to glory in the here and now and to the fame of it in future time.

When the Greek leaders approach Achilles in their attempt to persuade him to put an end to his quarrel with Agamemnon, they find him in his tent singing of the famous deeds of heroes to the accompaniment of his lyre (Book 6, lines 186ff.). In conversation with them, Achilles recounts his heroic choice in being at Troy; his goddess mother reported that destiny had given him two possibilities, he could choose either a long undistinguished life or, if he fought at Troy, a short life with undying fame (Book 6, lines 411ff.). As he is facing Achilles in their final encounter, Hector hopes to die while performing an heroic act that will meet the ears of men in future time (Book 22, lines 304–5). Achilles and Hector achieve their aspiration through the offices of the poet; Homer has immortalised them and through the *Iliad*, a poem that touches on many aspects of the Trojan story (Ilium being another name for Troy), he has given the world one of its most famous stories with a galaxy of characters in both the human sphere and the divine. For in the *Iliad* is the most famous representation of the gods and goddesses of Greek mythology, magnifying, intensifying and highlighting the heroic action by their councils and interventions whether solemn or comic.

Yet though we hear of the abduction of Helen that started the war and though the fall of Troy is clearly prophesied, Homer does not tell us the whole of the story from the beginning to the end. Within the larger Trojan story, he concentrates on a small part of it that covers some forty days in the ninth year of the siege; he has a particular theme signalled in the introductory lines that has to do with the anger of Achilles. In this concentration and particularisation lies the great artistry of the poem. Though it has breadth and scale almost like no other **epic**, it also has concentration and depth. And in this concentration on the anger of Achilles, Homer probes the values and attitudes of his hero, going beyond a depiction of conventional heroism, for Achilles undergoes an experience in the course of the poem that causes him to become disillusioned and causes the audience to feel that pity and fear which Aristotle later associated with **tragedy** in his famous analysis in his *Poetics*.

A tragic sense of life is distinctively Greek and is implicit in the myths which Homer inherited. The Olympian gods, created in man's image, are imaginative creations that express a **sublime** belief in human powers and physical beauty. They are created from the consciousness that beauty and excellence in the here and now are the summit of human aspiration. There is no compensating belief in a future reward after death, for Hades is an insubstantial world of twilight consciousness; nor is there in Greek myth a belief in the purposeful working out of the divine will in human history. Troy does not fall because of the righteous anger of Zeus. He has no quarrel with the Trojans who are one of his favourite peoples. Zeus himself must submit to fate, even though he would like to save his son Sarpedon (Book 16, lines 431–61). At the same time the Olympian gods express an acute awareness that man is a prey to conflicting amoral forces beyond human control. In this dual consciousness of the potential excellence of human capacities and their vulnerability to capricious and arbitrary powers is the potential for tragedy. This general potential is actualised in the particular experience of Achilles as the poet has organised and represented it in the poem.

It is this tragic sense of life that makes the poem an expression of great humanity and prevents it from ever being justifiably reckoned to be merely a celebration of man-killing brutes, even by those readers who have little sympathy with ancient ideas of heroism. In truth we do not need to share the ideals and attitudes of archaic Greece to respond to the *Iliad* and feel its greatness. And its energy is irresistible. Here is the testimony of one of Homer's greatest translators, the English poet Alexander Pope (1688–1744) writing in the preface to his translation in 1715:

> It is to the strength of this amazing invention we are to attribute that unequal fire and rapture, which is so forcible in Homer, that no man of a true poetical spirit, is master of himself while he reads him. What he writes is of the most animated nature imaginable; everything moves, everything lives, and is put in action. If a council be called, or a battle fought, you are not coldly informed of what was said

> or done as from a third person; the reader is hurried out of himself by the force of the poet's imagination, and turns in one place to a hearer, in another to a spectator.

Much of this energy can be felt even in a translation into modern prose.

When the god Hephaestus forges new armour for Achilles, the poet gives us an extended description of the mighty shield and of the various images engraved upon it by the god. He begins by describing pictures of two beautiful cities, a city at peace and a city at war. In the city at war is a battle in which the soldiers fight and drag off their dead like real living men (Book 18, line 539). The picture is beautiful not because the poet thinks war is a fine thing, but because the representation of it is realistic, life-like and vivid. Throughout the description of the shield, it is apparent that the poet appreciates the artistry of his fellow artist, the divine artificer, admiring his ability to highlight features and make the most of his materials, in this case different metals, so that important details stand out in relief. As well as providing a vivid description of the finished product, in the emphasis given to the process of manufacture the description of the shield is a portrait and celebration of the artist as god.

The subordination of the parts to a unifying theme, the tragic vision embodied within the epic through the experience of its hero, and the elevation of the immortal and immortalising artist as hero (as distinct from the prophet or priest), these are all expressions of the Greek spirit not simply apparent in an early form but fully developed in Homer.

In a poem that has been so widely read over such a long period, there will naturally be dissident voices and reservations expressed. Many serious-minded readers have been affronted by the frequent frivolity of Homer's gods and many readers who desire to look up to their heroes in straightforward admiration have been disappointed in Achilles and found him an unsympathetic figure. Not all readers have admired the way the main plot of the poem is prolonged and retarded; some have felt confused or wondered if several stories have been rather clumsily stitched together.

Over all hangs the troubling Homeric Question. Who was Homer, and when and where did he live? Could poems of this length be composed without the aid of writing? Is what we have the result of later editing? If early and late material can be identified, was the late material added to a lesser Homeric core? If we cannot determine the answers to some these questions, what exactly are we dealing with?

PART TWO

COMMENTARIES

There have been many editions of the Iliad *since the first edition printed in Florence in 1488. A reliable modern text of the Greek is the Oxford Classical Text of the* Iliad, *edited by T.W. Allen in three volumes, published by the Clarendon Press, Oxford, in 1931.*

In the preparation of this Note intended primarily for students reading a translation, the following version has been used: Homer: The Iliad *translated by E.V. Rieu, Penguin Books, Harmondsworth, 1950, and constantly reprinted. This edition has the line numbers of the Greek at the top of each page. Quotations in this Note are all from the above edition; line numbers, however, refer to the original Greek, so that it should be possible to use this Note easily with any reasonably literal version or any version where the lines of the original Greek are indicated. Greek names are given in the form in which they appear in this Penguin version: that is, for example, Achilles, rather than Akilleus.*

SYNOPSIS

The poet calls upon the Muse to sing of the fatal anger of Achilles that brought countless woes to the Greeks and sent many noble souls of heroes to Hades before their time, in fulfilment of the will of Zeus, after the quarrel broke out between Agamemnon, leader of the Greeks, and Achilles, their greatest fighter.

It is the ninth year of the siege of Troy. The god Apollo is angry because Agamemnon will not restore for ransom the daughter of one of his priests, captured before the siege of Troy, whom the Greek leader had taken as his prize in the general allotment of spoils. Apollo has sent a plague to infest the Greek camp. In a council called by Achilles to determine a course of action, Agamemnon quarrels with Achilles. He agrees to give up his prize, but takes steps to make up his loss by depriving Achilles of his spoil of war, the girl Briseis. Thus slighted,

Achilles withdraws from the fighting. He asks his goddess mother Thetis to persuade Zeus to grant the Trojans success, so that the Greeks will be forced to recognise his worth. In a council upon Olympus, Zeus agrees to Thetis's request (Book 1).

In the night Zeus sends a false dream of encouragement to Agamemnon, who then tests the army. After a council, the forces on both sides are marshalled and described (Book 2). Paris and Menelaus fight a duel (Book 3). The truce agreed for this duel is broken by Pandarus. Agamemnon inspects his troops (Book 4). Diomedes distinguishes himself in the fighting (Book 5). Hector returns to the city to arrange for the Trojan women to propitiate Athene who has been helping Diomedes. He then returns to the battlefield, having said farewell to Andromache (Book 6). Hector and Aias fight a duel which is interrupted by nightfall. In the evening a truce is made and a day is taken for the burial of the dead. In the following evening and night the Greeks build a wall to protect their ships (Book 7).

The next day sees the purposeful intervention of Zeus. The Trojans advance and encamp on the plain (Book 8). Faced with this threat, the Greeks that same evening unsuccessfully petition Achilles (Book 9). During the night Odysseus and Diomedes reconnoitre the Trojan camp (Book 10). The next day, in spite of Agamemnon's early success, Zeus promises Hector victory until sunset. The leading Greeks are wounded (Book 11), and the Trojans break through the wall (Book 12). Zeus takes his eye off the fighting, and Poseidon encourages the Greeks. Idomeneus distinguishes himself (Book 13). Zeus is then lulled to sleep by Hera and the Greeks are able to forestall Trojan success again. Hector is wounded (Book 14). Zeus awakes and fortunes are again reversed. The Trojans led by Hector break through to the ships (Book 15). Achilles allows Patroclus to fight in his armour to save the ships. Patroclus kills Sarpedon, and is then killed by Hector (Book 16). In the struggle over the body of Patroclus, Menelaus distinguishes himself (Book 17). News of Patroclus's death reaches Achilles. He grieves with Thetis, who promises him new armour. At sunset Hector rejects the advice of Polydamus to withdraw to the city. During the night Hephaestus makes Achilles's armour, while the Greeks mourn Patroclus (Book 18).

Next morning Achilles is presented with his new armour. In an assembly he renounces his anger. Agamemnon apologises and Briseis is restored. Preparations are made for battle (Book 19). The fighting begins with Achilles dominant and the gods active on both sides (Book 20). Achilles presses the Trojans back to the river and fights with Scamander (Book 21). Before the walls of Troy Hector is killed and mourned by the Trojans (Book 22). In the evening there is a council and a meal in the Greek camp. That night the ghost of Patroclus appears to Achilles requesting burial. Next day Patroclus is buried and funeral games are held in his honour (Book 23). Achilles is sleepless. For the next eleven days at dawn he abuses Hector's corpse. On the twelfth Zeus orders him to desist. That night Priam visits his tent with a ransom for Hector. Achilles allows a truce for burial. The Trojans collect wood for nine days and on the next day Hector is buried (Book 24).

DETAILED SUMMARIES

BOOK 1 **Achilles and Agamemnon quarrel. Achilles withdraws from the fighting. Zeus grants Thetis's request that the Greeks should suffer in the absence of Achilles**

See the first two paragraphs of the general summary for a summary of this book.

The poet announces his theme in the proposition by addressing his muse and bidding her sing of the anger of Achilles. This anger (the first word of the poem in the Greek) is described as destructive or pernicious ('fatal' in Rieu's translation) as it is the cause of many deaths; nevertheless, in the quarrel scene in which it begins it is clear that Achilles is sorely provoked and that Agamemnon is chiefly to blame. In depriving Achilles of his legitimate prize of war he is undermining the honour code on which relations between the heroes are based. Agamemnon is haughty and abuses his position as leader of the expedition. As a leader he shows no tact or political sensitivity; it is not in the interests of the Greek cause to alienate their chief fighter. In Achilles's eyes Agamemnon abuses his power and is guilty of hubris, arrogant behaviour that offends the gods (line 203). He prays that Agamemnon will rue his folly in not honouring the best of the Greeks (lines 411–12). Both Nestor and

Athene take Achilles's side and when Thetis, the goddess mother of Achilles, appeals to Zeus on her son's behalf, the father of the gods grants her request that the Greeks be worsted in the fight, so that they may appreciate the worth of her son who has been slighted. This promise represents 'the will of Zeus' which is referred to in the opening proposition.

The scene on Olympus has a strong comic dimension. The heavenly quarrel echoes in less serious terms the quarrels of the mortal protagonists that have preceded it. Zeus and Here carry on like a domestic couple; he is clearly henpecked and alarmed at the prospect of her shrewish tongue. She knows he is a philanderer who behaves badly and needs watching. Their son has to keep the peace. Nevertheless, Zeus is awesome when he nods his assent to Thetis which shakes Olympus, and in their dealing with mortals the gods are powers to be reckoned with. There is no trace of humour when Apollo wreaks destruction in the Greek camp or when Athene descends to calm Achilles.

1 ***goddess*** the muse. At Book 1, line 603 Homer refers to the muses singing on Mount Olympus, where the gods dwell. According to later writers there were nine muses who were the daughters of Zeus and Memory, each presiding over one of the major arts

2 ***Achaeans*** the Greeks; later Achaia was simply a part of Greece, in the northern Peloponnese

3 ***Hades*** the underworld where the spirits of the dead dwell

5 ***the will of Zeus*** (line 2 in Rieu) Zeus is the son of Cronos, whose rule he overthrew, and parent of many of the other gods. He is the most powerful of the Olympians, often referred to as their king, and his special province is the upper air where he controls storms and clouds, and sends rain. His power is expressed in his thunderbolt. Another of his emblems is the eagle. At Book 1, line 523 Zeus accedes to the request of Thetis, the mother of Achilles, that her son be avenged for the dishonour done to him by Agamemnon

7 ***Agamemnon*** the leader of the Greek expedition against Troy

14 **chaplet** a fillet made of wool; when wound around a staff it was a sign of the suppliant or one who was a priest. Suppliants and priests were protected by the gods

Book 1 continued

16 **the sons of Atreus** Agamemnon and Menelaus

18 **Olympus** a high mountain on the Greek mainland where it was believed the gods dwelt

30 **Argos** Greece generally, not merely the town of Argos

38 **Chryse, Cilla, Tenedos** all places near Troy. Tenedos is an island

39 **Smintheus** only occurs here, meaning possibly killer of mice

42 **Danaans** the Greeks (also called Achaeans or Argives)

43 **Phoebus** means 'shining', an appropriate **epithet** of the sun god; his sister Artemis, the moon goddess, is also called Phoebe

55 **white-armed goddess** the epithet probably suggests beauty. Here is the wife and sister of Zeus. She is a powerful goddess who supports the Greek cause as a result of the judgement of Paris (see Book 24, lines 25–30). Zeus gave Paris, the second son of King Priam of Troy, the task of deciding which of the three senior goddesses, Here, Athene and Aphrodite, was the fairest. Here offered Paris wealth and power, Athene offered him renown in war and Aphrodite offered him the most beautiful woman in the world, Helen, wife of the Greek Menelaus. Paris chose Aphrodite and her gift. This judgement not only offended Here and Athene but caused the Trojan War. The Greeks sent an expedition to recover Helen after Paris had abducted her to Troy

69 **an augur** one who tells the future (usually by observing the behaviour of birds), a prophet

118 **another prize** when the Greeks sacked cities it was customary to divide the spoils of war (women, horses, armour) among the victors according to status and merit. As these prizes were a mark of honour, it is natural that Agamemnon should demand a replacement. The link between prizes and honour is crucial to the outbreak of the quarrel

125 **captured towns** compare line 366 and also Book 6, line 415 and Book 9, lines 328–9

155 **Phthia** Achilles's homeland in Thessaly in northern Greece

180 **Myrmidons** the Thessalian people of whom Achilles was chief. The word is derived from the Greek word for ant. Zeus had created men from ants for Achilles's grandfather Aeacus, who was alone without a people

194 **Athene** the virgin warrior goddess who sprang from the head of Zeus. Her flashing eyes denote spirit and power

202 **aegis-bearing Zeus** the aegis is a heavy shield with a hundred gold tassels, the means of raising tempests and creating panic among mortals (see Book 5, line 738)

224 **Atreides** -ides means 'son of'. The son of Atreus, Agamemnon

242 **Hector** the chief warrior among the Trojans, as Achilles is the chief warrior among the Greeks

247 **Nestor** a wise old man, if somewhat garrulous. He is king of Pylos in the eastern Peloponnese

263 **Peirithous and Dryas** these older heroes took part in the battle between the Lapiths and the Centaurs, the latter a race of creatures half man half horse. Nestor makes the distinction between the two leaders clear. Agamemnon has greater prestige because he rules over more people; Achilles is the stronger and owes his strength to his goddess mother Thetis, a sea nymph daughter of Nereus

403 **Briareus** his father was Uranus, Sky

405 **Son of Cronos** Zeus, who deposed his father. Relations between the gods were not often harmonious. There is no other reference to this story in Homer or elsewhere

416 **so short a life** his mother told Achilles that he was fated either to gain glory and die early or to live a long but inglorious life. Achilles chose glory and knew that he would not return from the Trojan War (see Book 9, lines 410–16). Given this choice, any loss of honour was especially difficult to bear

423 **Ocean Stream** in Homer it was thought to encircle the earth

423 **Ethiopians** from the Homeric point of view they were a remote people living at the edge of the world

460 **slices from the thighs** these, wrapped in fat and soaked in wine, were offered to the gods

500 **clinging to his knees** Thetis adopts the usual mode of supplication

529 **The ambrosial locks** ambrosial means 'immortal'. Ambrosia is the food of the gods, nectar their drink

571 **Hephaestus** the god of fire and of metalwork. He makes the armour of Achilles in Book 18

593 **Lemnos** an island in the Aegean Sea

599 **laughter seized the happy gods** a famous comic moment

BOOK 2 Zeus sends a false dream. Agamemnon tests the army. There follows the Catalogue of Ships

Zeus sends a false dream to Agamemnon to tell him that he can now take Troy. Agamemnon decides to test his troops by telling them that he has been told by Zeus that his cause is lost. The soldiers rush to the ships and have to be rallied by Odysseus. There follows a council in which Thersites, a common soldier, rails against Agamemnon, and is beaten by Odysseus who restores good morale. Nestor advises Agamemnon to marshal his troops and there follows a long catalogue of the forces of the Greeks, and of the Trojans they face.

Book 2 extends the scope of the present action by suggesting its wider context (when, at the opening, Agamemnon talks of the nine-year siege of Troy) and by introducing a catalogue of forces at the end. The unstable situation in the Greek camp is further dramatised in the folly of Agamemnon's test and the subsequent flight of the army. Agamemnon's temperamental instability, his inept leadership and Nestor's role as the experienced old sage (all apparent in the quarrel scene of the opening book) are further confirmed in this scene. Odysseus, a man of sharp intelligence and a special favourite of Athene (the most sharp-witted of the goddesses), is introduced as a self-possessed, wily and capable character, in direct contrast to Agamemnon and in indirect contrast to Achilles. The council in which Thersites rails against Agamemnon, besides being of great dramatic interest in itself, re-enacts the quarrel scene of Book 1, with Agamemnon again maligned. Finally, the catalogue of forces widens the scale of the poem from a quarrel between a few individuals to involve the whole Mediterranean world. The number and range of **similes** at the opening of the catalogue have often been remarked upon.

6 **a False Dream** Homer has been much criticised for allowing Zeus to engage in such a wilful deception

42 **tunic** a close-fitting shift made of linen which reached below the knees. A large woollen cloak thrown over the shoulders was worn out of doors

51 **Assembly** this is the clearest picture in the poem of prevailing Greek institutions consisting of three parts: the king, the council of elders and the assembly of the whole people

73 **I am going to test them** it is difficult to say why Agamemnon should have decided to do this

101 **a staff** the description of its ancestry adds to the dignity of its possessor and confirms the close relation between gods and kings

Hermes the messenger of the gods. He guides Priam to the tent of Achilles in the final book

Argus a monster with a hundred eyes whom the suspicious Here had ordered to watch Io, a maiden beloved by Zeus whom Zeus had turned into a cow to avoid detection by Here

Pelops won his wife Hippodamia in a chariot race

Thyestes the brother of Atreus, father of Agamemnon

212 **Thersites** the only commoner to play a part in the poem. His physical deformity sets him apart from the rest of the heroes as does his abusive behaviour. He taunts Agamemnon in a manner similar to that of Achilles in Book 1, and calls to mind the quarrel between the two leading Greeks. A famous episode

260 **Telemachus** the young son whom Odysseus left behind when he went to Troy. He figures prominently in the *Odyssey*, especially in Books 1–4

303 **Aulis** a coastal town in Boeotia in northern Greece. Here in later accounts (though not in Homer) Agamemnon was forced to sacrifice his daughter Iphigeneia to the goddess Artemis in order to gain a favourable wind to sail for Troy

465 **Scamander** the river that has its source on Mount Ida and flows through the plain of Troy, sometimes called Xanthos, 'the yellow river'

484 **It was as bright as** the similes which introduce the catalogue are justly famous. The catalogue itself has been much discussed by commentators ancient and modern. In some manuscripts it is found with a separate heading; in others it is omitted altogether. Scholars agree that it is genuine and is of early origin, transmitting information from Mycenaean times. Whether it is a poetic fiction or a true historical record has been much debated. It has the effect of widening the scope of the poem to include much of the then known Greek world. Homer starts with the Boeotians in central Greece and moves south to the Peloponnese, then to the western islands, whence to Crete and the southern islands of the Aegean and back to the mainland. The total number of ships is more than 1,000

595 **Thamyris** a mythological excursus is inserted into the list as a diverting aside. A challenge to the gods brings its inevitable penalty

653 **Heracles** the most famous Greek hero of an earlier generation

690 **Lyrnessus** it is near Thebe, already mentioned by Achilles (Book 1, line 366)

718 **Philoctetes** later writers tell how Troy could only be taken with his bow and arrows, which had been a present from Heracles

755 **Styx** a river in Hades (meaning 'hate') by which the gods swear inviolable oaths

768 **Telamonian Aias** there are two Greeks called Aias or Aiax (or sometimes Aias) in Homer. The other is the son of Oileus

790 **Iris** a messenger of the gods who often takes the form of a rainbow. Here she takes the form of a mortal

BOOK 3 A truce is organised. King Priam describes the Greek heroes to Helen. Paris and Menelaus fight a duel

The two armies meet on the Trojan plain. Paris challenges the Greeks to single combat. Menelaus takes up the challenge, and Paris momentarily retires daunted. Hector upbraids Paris who then proposes a truce and a formal duel between himself and Menelaus to settle the issue of the war between them. Hector sends messengers to summon Priam. From the walls of Troy, Helen shows Priam the Greek leaders. A truce is made and oaths are taken. In the duel Menelaus defeats Paris who is rescued by Aphrodite and returned to Troy. Aphrodite summons Helen to Paris. Recriminations follow. Agamemnon proclaims Menelaus victor.

The scene changes to Troy and establishes both the main Trojan characters and the current climate of feeling in the city. At the same time the action involving Paris, Helen and Menelaus and the presence of Aphrodite puts before us the protagonists of the original quarrel and indirectly recounts the causes of the war. The scene between Priam and Helen gives brief character sketches of the Greeks and also establishes Helen's peerless beauty and her comparative innocence in Trojan eyes. Realistically, Helen must have known all that Priam tells her about the Greeks; this is the poet's way of introducing his characters to the audience. Helen's beauty is not directly described but famously represented in the reaction of the old men of Troy who say she is like an immortal goddess and that it is no marvel that the war is being fought over her. In Hector and Paris we have two contrasting characters, one dutiful, the other pleasure-loving. In the abduction of Helen from Sparta that started the war, Paris, it seems, is regarded as the guilty party, an inference further confirmed by his defeat in the duel. Later the refusal of Paris to give up Helen in Book 7 suggests the impasse which had led to the war. Helen is represented throughout in a sympathetic light (in contrast to many representations of her in later literature). The superiority of Menelaus over Paris here (and that of Aias over Hector in the duels of Books 3 and 8) suggests Trojan inferiority even without Achilles.

6 **Pigmies** the battle of the cranes and the pigmies (a people of small size) supposedly took place annually with the winter migration of the cranes to the warmer climate of Africa, in the Homeric world view a land at the edge of the earth

84 **The troops abandoned their attack** the challenge and the duel are chivalrously conducted according to set formulae, involving oath-taking, sacrifice and prayer. Both Greeks and Trojans observe the same code of battle, have the same religious ritual and arm themselves in the same way

125 **a great purple web** weaving is a traditional activity for women in Homer. Andromache is weaving when she hears news of Hector's death

145 **the Scaean Gate** on the western side of Troy facing the sea. The famous scene that follows is often called the Teichoscopia, the world-view from the wall

151 **like cicadas** a grasshopper, a famous **simile**

164 **I bear you no ill will at all** Priam blames the gods, not Helen. In reply Helen seems to accept responsibility for her part in the abduction

184 **Phrygia** a region east of Troy. The Amazons were women warriors who sometimes cut off their right breasts in order to use the bow more efficiently. They lived near the Caucasus

203 **Antenor added something to Helen's picture of Odysseus** before the war, Odysseus had visited Troy with Menelaus to try to regain Helen by peaceful means (compare Book 9, line 124 where it is said that Paris bribed the negotiators to reject Greek overtures)

210 **Menelaus** here characterised as being a man of few words. He came from Sparta in Laconia. The Spartans were famous for their taciturnity; whence the meaning of the word 'laconic'

238 **my own brothers** Helen does not know that they are already dead. Homer rarely intervenes in his own narrative and, when he does so, it is usually as here for **ironic** or **pathetic** effect

278 **you Powers of the world … pay for perjury** in spite of this there is little indication that the gods punished mortals in life or after death for breaking oaths. In the Homeric afterlife what survives is only the faintest shadow of a man, incapable of feeling joy or pain

330 **greaves** pieces of armour which protect the legs from the ankles to the knees

332 **cuirass** breastplate

380 **Aphrodite used her powers once more** the gods intervene in battle scenes as in every aspect of life in Homer. Paris is Aphrodite's favourite as a result of the Judgement of Paris explained above. She is the goddess of beauty as well as of love so that her devotee Paris is himself handsome, dresses well and is described in beautiful surroundings (notice his perfumed bedroom)

389 **Aphrodite … in the disguise of an old woman** the disguise of the goddess is to conceal her from others. Helen's initial refusal to obey her creates sympathy for her and underlines Aphrodite's power. The love goddess is not only seductive but threatening

401 **Maeonia** like Phrygia it lies east of Troy, even further from Helen's native Greece

BOOK 4 The truce is broken. Agamemnon marshals his troops

In a council upon Olympus, to annoy Here Zeus proposes that the terms of the truce be honoured and the war ended with Menelaus's victory. Here opposes this. The gods agree to arrange for the truce to be broken. Athene in disguise persuades Pandarus to shoot Menelaus with an arrow. He is wounded. Agamemnon marshals his troops and the armies engage.

The breaking of the truce by Pandarus is an act of treachery paralleling the original duplicity of Paris and perhaps putting the whole Trojan cause in a morally questionable light. The main heroes, like Menelaus and Paris in this instance, usually face each other with sword and spear; the use of a bow and arrow is regarded as underhand and beneath the dignity of a true warrior (see line 242. Later literature records that Paris, whose credentials as a warrior are called into question by his brother Hector, killed Achilles by means of an arrow directed at his heel, his one point of vulnerability). However, the issue is complicated by the fact that the breaking of the truce is organised by the gods. Athene puts the idea into the mind of Pandarus. Since Athene is the goddess of wisdom and reason, this prompting may in part be regarded as an **allegorical** representation of operations of the working of the mind. The squabbling and bartering of the gods in their council put them in a very bad light; they behave childishly and appear to have no concern other than to advance their own whims and pleasures. By way of contrast, Agamemnon, who hitherto has been seen to be both arrogant and weak, shows courage and leadership in responding to the wounding of Menelaus and in marshalling his troops.

2 **Hebe** daughter of Zeus and Here. Her name denotes youthful beauty. She is cupbearer to the gods

8 **Alalkomenean** the meaning of the word is not known

46 **the nearest to my heart was holy Ilium** Zeus here shows no hostility to the Trojans. On the contrary he approves of their piety. Nor does he show any sign of taking the serious view of their perjury held by the Greeks

88 **Pandarus** comes from Lycia, a region south-east of Troy famous for its archers and for the shrine of Apollo at Patara

105 **the bow** the arrowhead is of iron. Most weapons in Homer are made of bronze

133 **the corslet** made of two curved plates of bronze, one for the breast and one for the back, which overlapped at each side. They were kept in place with a clasp at the shoulder and with a belt at the waist. The arrow landed on the golden buckle of the belt where it lay over the two overlapping edges of the breast and back plates. Below the corselet was a girdle of metal plates lined with wool which further protected the waist and abdomen. The **apron**, made of leather, was beneath the girdle and covered the lower abdomen and upper thighs

142 **Carian or Maeonian** from regions far to the south and east of Troy

164 **The day will come** Agamemnon's prediction that Troy will fall is echoed by Hector at Book 6, line 448

204 **Asclepius** a son of Apollo, god of healing

Book 4 continued

219 **Cheiron** a centaur, half horse, half man, famous for his knowledge and wisdom. He taught the young Achilles and several other Greek heroes

307 **Those are the best tactics** the experienced old soldier persistently gives advice to Agamemnon, first in the opening quarrel, when the army has regrouped after fleeing to the ships, and now here in the matter of strategy. In fact the fighting subsequently centres upon the exploits of individual heroes. There is no attempt to keep in line as Nestor suggests

319 **Ereuthalion** see Book 7, line 136

358 **Odysseus, arch intriguer** although Agamemnon withdraws his insult, this is a further indication of his quick temper and bad judgement

372 **Tydeus** one of the seven heroes, the 'seven against Thebes', who tried to restore Polyneices, one of the sons of Oedipus, to Thebes after he had been expelled by his brother Eteocles who refused to share the kingship with him

Asopus a river south of Thebes

403 **Capaneus** another of the famous seven against Thebes which was eventually captured by the sons of the seven

446 **The bosses of their shields** the protuberance at the shield's centre

466 **to spoil him of his armour** it is an essential part of the fight that the killer should despoil the victim of his armour, not so much for its value, as for the visible prestige involved

474 **Simoïs** the second river of Troy, rising on Mount Ida and flowing into the Scamander

508 **Pergamus** the word means 'citadel', and is often used for the citadel of Troy where Apollo had a temple

BOOK 5 Diomedes's exploits are successful against the Trojans. He wounds Aphrodite

Diomedes distinguishes himself. Inspired by Athene, he drives the Trojans before him. He is wounded by an arrow from Pandarus, but is strengthened and encouraged by Athene who removes mist from his eyes so that he can recognise the gods. She permits him to fight against Aphrodite. Diomedes encounters Pandarus whom he kills and Aeneas whom he wounds with a stone. Aphrodite rescues Aeneas, and is then herself wounded by Diomedes. Apollo and Ares now help the Trojans. Hector, rebuked by Sarpedon, revives the Trojans and Diomedes retreats. Athene rebukes him and together they wound Ares.

This is the first of a series of exploits centred upon a single hero, called in Greek an ***aristeia***. The single focus gives narrative unity to the fighting. Diversity comes through the dramatic encounters with the gods. A further marked interest in this narrative comes from the descriptions of horses and chariots associated with the gods; there are the divine horses of Tros (lines 220ff.), the immortal horses lent by Ares to Aphrodite (lines 358ff.), and the glittering description of Here's chariot (lines 722ff.). The death of Pandarus may perhaps be regarded as a just reward for his treachery and a foreshadowing of the greater Trojan disaster to come. We are reminded that even without Achilles the Greeks have great fighters, and Diomedes's success is a fitting prelude to the Trojan fears that follow in Book 6.

1 **Diomedes** this book contains his *aristeia*, that is a sequence of his brave deeds

51 **Artemis** sister of Apollo and the goddess of chastity and hunting. As Apollo is the sun god, Artemis is the moon goddess

59 **Meriones** Athene is the goddess of the mechanical arts and so favours Meriones, a carpenter

77 **the River-god Scamander** rivers in Homer are personified. Achilles fights Scamander in Book 21

132 **use your sharp bronze and wound her** Athene encourages Diomedes to fight against her rival Aphrodite: a mortal could not fight against an immortal without the support of another god

222 **the horses of the breed of Tros** a pair of divine horses descended from the north wind Boreas (whence they derived their speed) were given to Tros, an early king of Troy which took its name from him, in return for his son Ganymede, a beautiful youth beloved by Zeus and taken up to Olympus by him to be the cupbearer of the gods

247 **Anchises** the horses belonged to the successors of Tros. Anchises was the younger brother of Laomedon, father of Priam and king before him

330 **Cyprian Aphrodite** Aphrodite is associated with Cyprus because she came to the island soon after her birth

333 **Enyo** personification of the tumult of battle, a companion of Ares

338 **the Graces** three sisters who gave festive joy and were associated with refinement and beauty, and so appropriate robe-makers to the goddess of beauty and love

385 **Otus and the mighty Ephialtes** these giants piled Pelion on Ossa and Ossa on Olympus (all mountains) in order to storm heaven (see *Odyssey*, Book 9, line 308). They were killed by Apollo. The Olympians had come to power by force

392 **Here ... Heracles** Heracles was a son of Zeus by Alcmene. His stepmother Here hated him from birth; she sent two snakes to kill him in his cradle. Heracles strangled them

395 **Hades** not only the kingdom of the dead but also the king himself. One of Heracles's labours was the task of fetching Cerberus, the three-headed dog, who guarded the entrance to the underworld

401 **Paeeon** in Greek the name means 'he who heals'

412 **Adrastus** one of the seven against Thebes. There is no other mention in Homer of the fate of Diomedes. In other writers he is one of the few Greeks to return home unscathed

447 **Leto** the mother of Apollo and Artemis

461 **Ares** particularly associated with Thrace, so that it is appropriate that he should take the form of a Thracian captain

500 **Demeter** the goddess of agriculture; not often mentioned in Homer

545 **River Alpheus** in the Peloponnese

576 **Pylaemenes** killed here, he is alive in Book 13 where he mourns the death of his son

629 **Sarpedon** a son of Zeus. His death in Book 16 is foreshadowed here

638 **Heracles** he saved Hesione, the daughter of Laomedon, king of Troy. He then attacked and captured Troy because the king failed to give him his promised reward, mares from the stock of the horses of Tros

741 **a Gorgon's head** the sight of the Gorgon Medusa was so terrible that she turned to stone all who looked upon her. She was slain by Perseus with the help of a mirror provided by Athene

785 **Stentor** means in Greek 'roarer' from which the English 'stentorian'

789 **Dardanian** Trojan: Dardanus was one of the founders of the Trojan race

897 **the Sons of Uranus** probably refers to the Titans whom the Olympian gods displaced

BOOK 6 Diomedes encounters Glaucus; they chivalrously exchange armour. Hector bids farewell to Andromache

The continuing Greek success prompts Helenus to advise his brother Hector to persuade the Trojan women to propitiate Athene. On the battlefield Diomedes encounters Glaucus and on recognising that they are hereditary guest friends, they exchange armour and part in friendship. Meanwhile Hector delivers his message to Hecabe, and goes to the house of Paris to persuade him to fight. Helen also rebukes Paris. Hector then meets Andromache with their son on the tower and bids farewell to her before returning together with Paris to the fighting.

The encounter between Glaucus and Diomedes is highly chivalric and illustrates the obligations of guest friendship, part of the Homeric honour code that embraces Greek and Trojan alike. The long narrative of Glaucus involving tales of past heroism has been censured on the grounds of improbability but the *Iliad* is not a realistic narrative like a nineteenth-century novel. The narrative is diversified with the contrasting tales of past heroes.

While the first Trojan scene in Book 3 recalls the past, the second major Trojan scene here looks ominously to the future. The parting of Hector and Andromache firmly establishes Hector as the mainstay of the Trojan cause upon whom all will depend and is full of foreboding for his fate and that of the city with which he is identified. There is much **irony** and **pathos** in this scene; the incident involving the fright of the young child at the nodding plume of his father's helmet and the consequent laughter of the parents in the middle of their tearful farewell has always been regarded as one of the most human and affecting moments of the poem.

90 **Let her choose a robe** on the frieze of the temple of the Parthenon on the Athenian Acropolis there is a depiction of the presentation of the sacred robe (the peplos) to Athene

119 **Diomedes** given that he has just wounded Aphrodite and Ares, it is strange that Diomedes tells Glaucus that he will not fight against him if he proves to be a god. The apparent inconsistency has been much debated, but

Athene, while encouraging him to fight Aphrodite, had expressly forbidden him to fight with other gods (see Book 5, lines 129–30)

132 **Dionysus** the god of wine and intoxication. He was brought up in a cave near Mount Nysa in Thrace

146 **Men in their generations are like the leaves of the trees** these lines are among the most celebrated in Homer

154 **Sisyphus** his wickedness in life was punished in the underworld where he had to roll uphill a huge stone which rolled back every time it reached the top

169 **a folded tablet** the only reference in Homer to anything that could be a kind of writing

179 **the Chimaera** the only example in Homer of a hybrid monster. Bellerophon's exploits represent a different kind of heroism from that celebrated in the *Iliad*. His tasks are like the labours of Heracles, who cleansed the earth of assorted monsters. Homer does not mention the winged horse Pegasus with which Bellerophon is associated in later writers

208 **Strive to be best** a famous line repeated at Book 11, line 784 where it is advice given by Peleus to Achilles

236 **golden armour for bronze** this line became proverbial. The two heroes chivalrously feel the inherited obligations of guest friendship. An exchange of gifts was customary. Compare also the exchange of gifts between Hector and Aias at Book 7, lines 290–2

291 **Sidon** in Phoenicia, a region of developed culture. The Phoenicians were great traders

316 **eleven cubits** a sixteen-foot spear

317 **Acropolis** the high point of the city

403 **'Astyanax'** the name means 'leader of the city'. The name Hector means 'defender'. In later literature it is recorded that Astyanax was thrown off the battlements of Troy by Odysseus; there is no indication of this abominable fate in Homer

416 **Eëtion** referred to at Book 1, line 364

417 **he was too chivalrous to despoil him** here Achilles follows the usual heroic code in allowing burial to an enemy. The contrast with his treatment of Hector is foreshadowed

438 **Someone who knows the oracles ... its history** according to some accounts, when Poseidon and Apollo built the walls of Troy, a mortal helped them at one point; here only the walls might be breached

448 **the day … when holy Ilium will be destroyed** Hector's prophecy echoes Agamemnon's at Book 4, lines 163–5. Compare his earlier foreboding at lines 366–7

491 **the loom and the spindle** in Homeric society the sexes have very distinct roles

506 **like a stallion** the **simile** is repeated with reference to Hector at Book 15, lines 263–8

BOOK 7 Hector and Aias fight a duel. Both sides bury their dead

Hector issues a challenge to single combat. The Greeks draw lots and Aias confronts Hector. In the fight Aias gets the better of Hector. Heralds from both sides intervene; the heroes stop fighting and exchange gifts. That evening Nestor proposes a truce for the burial of the dead. In Troy Antenor advises the return of Helen and her property. Paris will not let Helen go, but is prepared to surrender her goods. The Greeks reject the Trojan offer but agree to a truce for the burial of the dead. They also decide to dig a trench and build a high wall to protect their ships.

The duel between Aias and Hector foreshadows the later duel between Achilles and Hector, which will be the climax of the poem. This is a fierce encounter but is nevertheless fought chivalrously according to the rules of Homeric warfare. Hector's conditions at the start, relating to the restoration of the corpse of the loser for proper burial of the dead, assert one of the basic norms of Homeric civilisation which is later to be violated by Achilles who seeks to deny him burial. This duel therefore not only foreshadows the later encounter but also clearly establishes the norm from which the latter departs. After the duel at the end of the day both sides agree to a truce for the burial of their dead, so that this book advances the plot by emphasising one of its main themes: respect for the traditional burial rites (without which it was believed the soul could not enter Hades) which are to be extended to the defeated enemy.

86 **Hellespont** the narrow strait between the Trojan plain and the Thracian Chersonese, now dividing Europe from Asia

125 **Peleus** see Book 9, line 765 where Nestor's visit to Peleus to recruit Achilles is referred to

149 **Ereuthalion** mentioned earlier by Nestor at Book 4, line 319. It is part of his character that he looks back to past exploits which he relates somewhat garrulously

194 **let your prayers be silent** the idea is to prevent the enemy using the same formula to counter-persuade the god in question. Characteristically Aias puts belief in his own powers before any such superstition

202 **Mount Ida** it rises to the east of Troy

221 **Hyle** in Boeotia

232 **start the fight** usually decided by lot, so that Hector feels affronted that Aias should give him an apparent advantage, thus asserting his own superiority

299 **let us exchange gifts of honour** such magnanimity is characteristic of Hector, the most chivalrous of the heroes at Troy

325 **a discussion was opened by the old man Nestor** there are two strange features of this speech. The custom of taking bones home (different from a communal burning) is not referred to elsewhere in Homer. As the Greeks are winning, it is not obvious why the proposal to build a defensive wall should be made here

355 **Prince Paris** the Trojans despise Paris and even the herald Idaeus boldly curses him, yet Paris is allowed a veto in matters that concern him

445 **Poseidon** the god of the sea, but also the god who can make the earth quake. He was cheated by Laomedon of his payment for building the walls of Troy. He opposes the Trojan cause

469 **Jason** an earlier hero, the leader of the Argonauts who had sailed after the golden fleece

BOOK 8 The Trojans advance to the wall which protects the Greek ships

On the second day of the fighting Zeus calls a council and forbids the gods to intervene on either side, saying that he is determined to bring the war to a close. From Mount Ida he encourages the Trojans, sending thunderbolts among the Greeks and causing them to flee before Hector. Here and Athene, who realise that Zeus is honouring his promise to Thetis, prepare to help the Greeks but are driven back in fright by Zeus's anger. Night falls, and the Trojans encamp on the battlefield in front of the newly built wall.

Trojan success (promised by Zeus) is the necessary prelude to the embassy to Achilles which follows in the next book.

13 **Tartarus** a place of punishment for rebellious gods; see lines 479–81

15 **a golden rope** a much **allegorised** passage

48 **Gargarus** the summit of Mount Ida

69 **golden scales** the scales of Zeus are a dramatic figurative expression for the workings of fate. Whether the notion implies a fate which is beyond the will of Zeus (rather than merely being its expression) has been much debated

75 **Zeus thundered out from Ida** the Trojan victory is brought about directly by the intervention of Zeus in fulfilment of his promise to Thetis given in Book 1. See also lines 133 and 170

203 **Helice and Aegae** both on the northern coast of the Peloponnese; notable shrines to Poseidon

247 **eagle** the bird of Zeus

284 **though a bastard child** when Heracles sacked Troy he took away Hesione and gave her as a slave to Telamon. Teucer was their offspring, his name indicating his Trojan descent

290 **a tripod** a three-legged kettle for warming water

349 **with the eyes of Gorgo** that is, with a look that inspires great terror

363 **Eurystheus** a king of Mycenae for whom Heracles performed his twelve labours

368 **Erebos** meaning 'darkness', another name for the underworld. Styx, the river of hate, is in Hades

479 **Iapetus and Cronos** Titans, sons of Uranus overthrown by the Olympians

554 **many fires alight** the night piece with which the book closes is much celebrated

BOOK 9 The Greeks try to persuade Achilles to relent

The Greeks are in a state of panic. Agamemnon calls an assembly and suggests flight. Diomedes rebukes him, and Nestor suggests a private council in which he proposes that they immediately propitiate Achilles. Agamemnon agrees, offering princely gifts and the restoration of Briseis. Aias, Odysseus, and Phoenix, Achilles's aged retainer, go by night to Achilles's tent to make the appeal. Achilles is not moved, and the ambassadors return to report failure.

The main heroes act very much in the character that has already been established. Nestor as usual offers practical advice for the immediate present. In his second speech he defines the obligations of the king (line 100ff.) and clearly blames Agamemnon for not having followed his advice in the initial quarrel. Agamemnon admits his folly but still wants Achilles to yield.

In addressing Achilles, the politic Odysseus repeats Agamemnon's offer verbatim, but tactfully omits Agamemnon's requirement that Achilles should submit. Odysseus cleverly reminds Achilles of the advice of his father Peleus that he should subdue his haughty spirit (*thumos*) for the sake of friendly feeling (*philosophrosune*) (lines 252–9) and skilfully saves his most persuasive appeal – to Achilles's desire for glory – until the end. In his unrelenting reply Achilles recalls the choice of destiny as given to him by his mother Thetis: that he could either have a short life with fame, or a long one without it. The insult to his honour makes it seem that his heroic choice is being nullified. In anger he renounces the heroic impulse that motivated him to fight at Troy.

The emotional appeal of Phoenix, Achilles's old retainer, who only appears in this scene, is to Achilles's reputation among the Greeks, something for which Achilles shows no regard. His verdict is that Agamemnon's gifts are generous, and go beyond what was required by form alone. He who does not show reverence (*aidos*) for the prayers that seek to undo the harm done by Ate will himself be undone (Book 9, lines 496–514). Achilles is now identified as the man of error, folly and delusion. His tale of Meleager offers the precedent of one who acted too late to be honoured by those he saved (lines 524–99).

Aias's blunt speech expresses the straightforwardness of his character. To him it seems a simple matter, for the social customs of the time allow for more serious offences (such as the killing of kin) to be paid for by compensation. In reply Achilles virtually admits that what Aias has said is fair but he cannot stomach the way he has been treated like a newcomer, that is, one who has no kin to avenge him. His last words show that he really has no intention of leaving for home. He will fight when Hector reaches his ship.

When news of his refusal is delivered to the Greek camp Diomedes speaks for them all (and perhaps for the audience) when he condemns his stubborn pride.

13 **Agamemnon rose to address them** repeated from Book 2, lines 110–18 and 139–41

31 **Diomedes** his reply refers back to Agamemnon's speech at Book 4, lines 370–400

145 **I have three daughters** Agamemnon says Achilles can have one of them as his bride without giving gifts; the usual practice was for the bridegroom to give large sums to the father of the bride. Agamemnon offers to reverse the practice

145 **Iphianassa** another name for Iphigeneia. This reference to her suggests that the story that Agamemnon sacrificed her at Aulis to appease the goddess Artemis who had becalmed the Greek fleet on the way to Troy (basic to the plot of *The Oresteian Trilogy* by the later poet Aeschylus) was not known to Homer

149 **seven fine towns** presumably tributary states. Agamemnon offers substantial gifts, but still requires that Achilles submit

189 **He was singing of famous men** Achilles's singing illustrates clearly the connection between the hero, fame and song

252 **Peleus** Odysseus and Nestor recruited Achilles from him for the war

381 **Orchomenos or ... Egyptian Thebes** both legendary for their wealth; the only mention of Egypt in the poem

404 **Rocky Pytho** Apollo's famous oracle at Delphi was called Pytho after the dragon killed there by Apollo. Rich offerings were brought to the oracle by those consulting it

478 **Hellas** not, as later, the whole of Greece, for which Homer's word is normally Achaia

502 **prayers** the only developed **allegory** in Homer. The prayers follow upon Ate which means 'folly' or 'infatuation' though it is often translated as 'sin', as penitence might follow upon wrongdoing. If the injured party listens to the prayers, he will be rewarded; if not, he too will be visited by Ate

543 **Meleäger** the story in which he features is the longest exemplary myth in Homer. The poet typically starts in the middle and then goes back in time. Calydon is in the north-west of Greece

562 **Alcyone** the Greek word for kingfisher

Books 6–10 continued

BOOK 10 Odysseus and Diomedes capture the Trojan spy Dolon in a night raid

That same night, the Greek camp being in further confusion, Nestor suggests that spies be sent to discover Trojan intentions. Odysseus and Diomedes volunteer. They capture the Trojan spy Dolon who has been sent by Hector on a similar errand, and he tells them of the prize horses of the newly arrived Thracian king Rhesus who is encamped nearby. Diomedes kills Dolon: the sleeping Rhesus and his followers are killed and his horses are captured.

This is the least heroic part of the poem. However, the night attack is realistic in that it is the kind of intelligence mission that occurs in warfare and the episode varies the action of the poem by offering something new.

257 **'skull-cap'** such an helmet like this of Odysseus is known to have been worn in the Mycenaean period only, and not subsequently. The description must have come down from a period before the poem was composed

267 **Autolycus** the grandfather of Odysseus

415 **Ilus** king of Troy, grandfather of Priam. Troy (Ilium) was named after him

457 **Dolon's head met the dust** the killing of an unarmed suppliant in such a manner has been thought beneath the dignity of an Homeric hero

467 **tamarisk** a marsh shrub

577 **they bathed themselves in polished baths ... rubbing themselves with olive-oil** the Greeks have with them the amenities of civilisation

BOOK 11 Agamemnon drives the Trojans back until he is wounded. Hector leads a counter-attack in which the leading Greeks are wounded

The Greeks, led by Agamemnon, push the Trojans back to the Scaean Gate. Hector is warned by Zeus to retreat until Agamemnon retires. Thereafter he is promised glory until sunset. Agamemnon is wounded. Hector returns and is checked by Diomedes who is then wounded by an arrow from Paris. Odysseus is wounded and retires. Hector advances, forcing the Greeks on to the defensive. Machaon, wounded by Paris, is taken back to the Greek camp by Nestor. Hector forces Aias to retire. Achilles sees Nestor returning with Machaon and sends Patroclus to discover who the wounded man is. Nestor advises Patroclus to persuade Achilles to send him and the Myrmidons to their aid.

The ***aristeia*** of Agamemnon shows the Greek leader in action for the first time. Whatever his weakness as a leader, he does not lack courage and physical strength.

Achilles's interest in the wounded shows that he is not indifferent to events and brings him again to the attention of the audience. Old Nestor's accounts of his exploits when young diversify the narrative and are very much in character. His account of the visit to Peleus when he and Odysseus had recruited Achilles for the war and of the words of Patroclus's father further advance the plot as Nestor suggests to Patroclus to prevail upon Achilles to let him fight wearing his armour. Once again Nestor offers crucial tactical advice.

1 **Tithonus** brother of Priam, he was given immortality by Zeus at the Dawn's request. She forgot to ask for eternal youthfulness. This is the third day of fighting after Achilles's withdrawal

20 **Cinyras** later famous as a king of Cyprus

36 **Gorgon's head** the three-headed monster has snakes for hair so that the description of the twisting enamel is particularly apt and artful

113 **as it is for a lion** Agamemnon, king of men, is compared four times to a lion, king of beasts. See lines 129, 173, 238

185 **Iris** Zeus promises Hector supremacy only until sunset. Hector forgets this limitation

270 **the Eileithyiae** meaning the twisters, daughters of Here, the goddess of childbirth

362 **Diomedes ... 'You cur'** his insulting words are repeated by Achilles at Book 20, lines 449–54

375 **Paris ... drew a bow** the contempt expressed by Diomedes for the bowman is felt throughout the poem where all the fighting is essentially hand-to-hand combat between armed warriors

403 **Odysseus was perturbed** his internal debate contrasts with the more physical reactions of Aias when similarly outnumbered later at line 548

548 **like a tawny lion** this **simile** is repeated at Book 17, lines 657–66

558 **as stubborn as a donkey** this simile has been much criticised on the grounds that it is demeaning for a hero to be compared to such a lowly beast. The juxtaposition of these two celebrated similes produces a striking effect

Book 11 continued

599 **Achilles ... called at once to his friend** Homer here advances the plot by making Achilles send Patroclus to Nestor who makes the fatal suggestion that leads to Patroclus's death (lines 796–803)

632 **a magnificent beaker** Nestor's cup closely resembles a golden cup discovered in the graves at Mycenae

647 **Patroclus** even his friend finds Achilles difficult. To the Greeks he is a thorn in their flesh as Paris is to the Trojans

670 **if only I were still as young ... as I was** as always Nestor looks to the past. He compares his unselfish valour with that of Achilles

690 **Heracles** here apparently a destructive figure

701 **Augeas** famous for his stables cleaned by Heracles as one of his labours

709 **the two Moliones** see Book 23, line 638

784 **always to strive for the foremost place and outdo his peers** Peleus's advice repeats that given to Glaucus at Book 6, line 208; it encapsulates both the heroic and competitive impulse that is the main motivation of Greeks and Trojans

832 **Cheiron** a centaur (half man, half horse) who educated Achilles

BOOK 12 Hector storms the wall and breaks into the Greek camp

The Trojans, led by Hector, cross the trench on foot and attempt to break through the wall. Sarpedon leads the decisive attack with Glaucus and the Lycians. Mnestheus, Aias and Teucer oppose them. Finally, Hector breaks the gate with a great stone, and leads the Trojans into the Greek camp.

This book contains two of the most celebrated speeches in the poem. In rejecting superstitious fears and omens and putting his faith in Zeus, Hector, on whose prowess his country depends, utters a famous patriotic sentiment 'Fight for your country – that is the best and only omen' (line 243). Soon after, the Trojan Sarpedon addressing Glaucus (lines 310ff.) offers a justification for their aristocratic privileges and in so doing gives the most explicit articulation of 'the heroic code' that binds and motivates Greeks and Trojans alike. It is a remarkable feature of 'many-minded Homer' that these two noble utterances should be made by the enemies of the Greeks.

4 **this wall for the ships** the failure to make proper offerings causes Apollo and Poseidon who had built the walls of Troy to destroy them

27 **Trident** a spear with three prongs which is the emblem of Poseidon's power

110 **Asius** his story is resumed at Book 13, line 384

128 **the warlike Lapith race** the Lapithae had fought a famous battle with the centaurs

210 **Polydamas** he bad offered advice that Hector had been pleased to take earlier (lines 60–80)

421 **like two men quarrelling** the **simile** implies a system of agriculture similar to the strip farming common in medieval Europe with equitable distribution of land among members of the community. The *Iliad* is notable for the variety of its similes

BOOK 13 The battle rages at the ships; Idomeneus worsts the Trojans whose advance is checked

Zeus turns his eyes from the battle. Poseidon comes to the aid of the Greeks. Idomeneus does great deeds. Hector confronts Aias. The Trojan advance is checked.

> This part of the fighting is marked by the opposition of Zeus and Poseidon who are working for and against the Trojans. Their opposition is encapsulated in a remarkable image: 'Thus the gods saw to it that the rope they had knotted for this desperate and even tug-of-war was tautened either way. The rope was unbreakable and no one could undo the knot; but it undid many a man' (lines 358–60).

5 **Mysians** these people came from the north, from southern Russia and the lower Danube

12 **Samothrace** an island north-west of Troy in the Thracian Sea. The plain of Troy can be seen from its high mountains

21 **Aegae** no such place near Troy has been identified by commentators

33 **Tenedos and rugged Imbros** islands off the coast of Troy

82 **joy of battle** the Greek word is *charma*. War is also regarded as hateful. There are many attitudes to war in the *Iliad*

111 **the whole blame does rest with our overlord Agamemnon** Poseidon blames Agamemnon: this recapitulates the main theme

Book 13 continued

171 **Imbrius** most of the Trojans whose deaths are dwelt upon are in some way related to Priam and the royal house

345 **the two mighty sons of Cronos, taking different sides** Poseidon and Zeus were both sons of Cronos and Rhea. Although Zeus has more power and knowledge than other Olympians, he is clearly neither omnipotent nor omniscient, even though sometimes he is addressed as such by other characters in the poem

366 **Cassandra** this tragic figure is mentioned only twice in the poem

460 **Aeneas always bore King Priam (a grudge)** no explanation is given for this in the poem

612 **a fine bronze axe** not used as a weapon elsewhere in Homer, nor is the sling referred to here

643 **Pylaemenes** already killed at Book 5, line 576

BOOK 14 When Zeus is deceived into sleep by Here, Trojan successes are reversed

The Greek leaders, nursing their wounds in the Greek camp, respond to the sound of the fighting with a new resolve, encouraged by Poseidon. Here borrows Aphrodite's girdle, obtains the help of Sleep and lulls Zeus to sleep on Mount Ida. Poseidon further encourages the Greeks. Hector is knocked unconscious by a stone thrown by Aias. The Trojans are driven back from the wall.

The deception of Zeus by Here (so that Poseidon can help the Greeks unhindered by Zeus who wants to fulfil his promise to Thetis by seeing the Greeks worsted) shows the gods again in a comic light and behaving in a very human way. The episode is one of the most sensual in Homer.

83 **'What fatal leadership!'** Odysseus's rebuke puts Agamemnon again in a bad light as a weak leader prone to depression

114 **Tydeus** migrated to Argos because he had killed someone, according to later accounts. Diomedes passes over the incident in silence

178 **Athene** as the goddess of the mechanical arts, she presides over spinning and weaving, and so makes a robe for Here

201 **Ocean ... and Mother Tethys** usually regarded as the children of Uranus (sky) and Earth. Here they seem to be primal beings

203 **Rhea** wife of Cronos who was ousted by Zeus

226 **Pierian range** a region in Thessaly bordering on Olympus

Emathia to the north of Pieria in Macedonia. Athos is a mountain on the Chalcidian peninsula. Lemnos is an island opposite Troy

250 **Heracles** see Book 5, line 640; Book 15, lines 18–30; Book 19, lines 96–133

275 **the young Graces** beautiful daughters of Zeus

279 **Titans** pre-Olympian gods who had been banished to Tartarus by Zeus

284 **Lecton** a southern spur of Mount Ida

317 **Ixion's wife** Dia

321 **daughter of Phoenix** Europa

326 **Demeter** by her Zeus was father of Persephone

327 **Leto** by her he was father of Apollo and Artemis

445 **Satnioïs** the river runs westward from Mount Ida

BOOK 15 When Zeus awakens, fortunes are reversed and the Greeks are pursued back to the ships

Zeus awakens, angrily rebukes Here, sends Iris to impose his will on Poseidon and sends Apollo to revive Hector so that he can drive the Greeks back to the ships. The Trojans advance, and Apollo fills in the trench and knocks down the wall. Hector is opposed by Aias with Teucer, Menelaus and Antilochus. The Greeks are forced back to the ships. In stubborn defence Aias leaps from ship to ship as the Trojans bring firebrands to Hector so that he can set fire to the ships.

Zeus's reply to Here (lines 53ff.) summarises the rest of the poem, making it clear that he will keep his promise to Thetis. Through the Olympian view provided by the gods the poet controls his narrative and reminds the audience of its outcome which is never in doubt. Zeus further goes on to relate Athene's part in the destruction of Troy. (She provided the inspiration for the stratagem of the wooden horse.) The use of prediction therefore skilfully alludes to the future and imparts an aura of inevitability and fateful purpose in contrast to the apparent confusion and chaos of the present action.

In his ***aristeia*** Hector is repeatedly associated in the imagery of the **similes** and surrounding narrative with the fire that he brings to the Greek ships.

14 **Here** the fettering of Here is referred to by Zeus at the end of Book 1. Nothing else is known about it

25 **Heracles** Here refers to the incident at Book 14, line 266

41 **it is due to no prompting of mine** she is almost telling the truth; see her words to Poseidon at Book 8, lines 201–11 and his reply

87 **Themis** her name means 'law and custom'

112 **Ascalaphus** his death is related at Book13, line 518

204 **the Avenging Furies** they avenge wrongs done to the family. In spite of Poseidon's account of the lottery, the older brother has the most power in heaven as on earth

263 **like a stallion** repeated from Book 6, lines 506–511 where it is applied to Paris not Hector as here

313 **the aegis** Apollo wields it on behalf of Zeus who never appears in person on the battlefield

390 **Patroclus** the poet returns to the scene described at the end of Book 11

614 **Pallas Athene** the goddess actually plays a part in Hector's death in Book 22

BOOK 16 Patroclus, wearing the armour of Achilles, kills Sarpedon and then is killed in turn by Hector

Achilles yields to Patroclus's plea and lets him put on the armour of Achilles and lead the Myrmidons in battle. Achilles warns him not to pursue Hector. Patroclus inspires the Greeks and extinguishes the fire that had broken out on one of their ships. The Trojans retreat before his advance. Sarpedon offers resistance but is slain by Patroclus. Glaucus rallies Hector and the Trojans to recover the body of Sarpedon. Zeus spirits the body away to Lycia. Patroclus presses on, heedless of Achilles's warning. He is struck by Apollo, wounded by Euphorbus and finally killed by Hector whose death he predicts in his last words.

This book, in which Achilles returns to the narrative, contains the pivotal action of the poem, the death of Patroclus, that causes Achilles to return to the fighting. Although Achilles sent Patroclus to find out about the wounded in Book 11, in fact he returns later on the same day.

When Patroclus remarks to the stubborn Achilles that while doctors are treating the leading Greeks, he alone is untreatable (lines 21–35), Achilles relents to the point of allowing Patroclus to fight in his place wearing his armour. Here are the first signs of a recognition of his error, as Achilles admits that a man cannot be angry for ever (lines 60–1). The concern for his honour is still overriding; Patroclus must only save the ships; he must not fight on to Troy or he will diminish the honour of Achilles (lines 80–90). But there is magnanimity as well as **irony** in his final wish that both he and Patroclus may survive to take Troy together (lines 97–100).

Sarpedon is the first great hero to die (line 502). His death is marked like that of other great heroes by much divine interest and a death speech. The moment when Zeus wonders whether to save his son Sarpedon (lines 435ff.) not only raises questions about the relationship between fate and the will of Zeus but increases the **pathos**. His tears of blood are a powerful image, showing the humanity of the gods in a sympathetic light. In his final speech addressed to his friend Glaucus, Sarpedon sustains the heroism and concern for honour and glory that had marked his earlier great speech in Book 12, lines 310ff.

Hector's taunting speech to the dying Patroclus about the vanity of his aspirations to sack Troy (lines 830ff.) and his assumption that Achilles had given him orders not to return till he had killed Hector are ironic and thus increase the dramatic effect, for Achilles had expressly forbidden Patroclus to attempt the sack of Troy (lines 89ff.), warning that his own honour would thereby be diminished and expressing the wish that they might take Troy together. These words remind us that Patroclus in leading his men towards Troy and pursuing Hector (lines 383ff.) brought disaster on himself by disobeying the orders of his friend. Hector's taunt and the dying Patroclus's prophecy (lines 852ff.) foreshadow the similar taunts and prophecy involving Achilles and Hector when Hector is slain in Book 22.

3 **Hot tears** Patroclus's tears repeated from Book 9, line 14, relating to Agamemnon

7 **like a little girl** compare the **simile** of the child who builds sandcastles on the shore at Book 15, line 362

36 **some prophecy** possibly referring to the two fates mentioned by Achilles at Book 9, line 410

38 **Then at least allow *me* to take the field** this recalls Nestor's speech at Book 11, lines 794–803

60 **But what is done cannot be undone** Achilles relents; in Book 9 he had said he would wait until the Trojans reached his own ships. But even now he does not fight himself

144 **Mount Pelion** in Thessaly not far from Phthia. Cheiron gave the spear to Peleus on his marriage to Thetis

149 **Xanthus** sometimes translated as 'tawny'; Balius – 'dapple', Pedasus – 'jumper', Podarges – 'gleaming feet' or 'swift feet'. Horses were often said to be descended from winds (because of their speed). The horses had been given to Peleus by Poseidon as a wedding present

153 **Eëtion's city** see Book 1, line 366 and Book 6, line 416

174 **Spercheus** a river in Thessaly. Nothing is known of Achilles's sister

202 **you called me a brute** Achilles refers here to the displeasure of the Myrmidons which is not described in the poem. This is unusual in Homer

233 **Pelasgian Zeus** the Pelasgians were the earliest inhabitants of Greece who established the worship of Dodonian Zeus. Zeus had an oracle at Dodona in Epirus

328 **Chimaera** the monster killed by Bellerophon and described at Book 6, lines 179–83

386 **Zeus sends down torrential rain as a punishment to men** the motivation in this simile implies a more moral Zeus than he generally appears to be in the *Iliad*

471 **the trace-horse** a third horse harnessed beside a pair to take the place of either of them in case of need. Pedarus is the mortal horse

BOOK 17 Menelaus distinguishes himself in the fight for the body of Patroclus

The fight continues over the body of Patroclus. Menelaus kills Euphorbus but retreats before Aias. Glaucus rebukes Hector who puts on Achilles's armour and encourages the Trojans. Aias and Menelaus exhort the Greeks. The Trojans gain the body but are beaten off by Aias. The battle continues until finally Menelaus and Meriones recover the body while the two Aiantes ward off the Trojans.

The **ironic** note continues when Glaucus, who does not know that Zeus has spirited away the body of Sarpedon, unjustly rebukes Hector. In the mêlée of the fighting, the protagonists do not share the Olympian view granted to the audience. Hector's reply that all mortals are at the mercy of Zeus (lines 176ff.) also contains more truth than he knows. The Olympian perspective is again used to **pathetic** effect when Zeus sadly remarks that Hector's triumph as he wears the armour of Achilles will be short-lived (lines 201ff.).

The confusion of the fighting and the fearful darkness that surrounds the central struggle around the body of Patroclus, together with the disquieting imagery featuring dogs and carrion birds all mark an intensification of the darkening emotional tone as the poem now moves towards its climax.

24 **Hyperenor** killed by Menelaus at Book 14, line 516

97 **Menelaus ... 'What shall I do?'** the Homeric heroes act not only upon impulse but with calculation

127 **the dogs of Troy** decent burial was a matter of honour and piety, since it was believed that the soul of the departed could not pass to the underworld without it. Hence Zeus is concerned about the burial of his son Sarpedon (Book 16, lines 667–75) and hence the particular horror of being exposed as carrion for dogs or crows (the idea recurs in this book, and with increasing emphasis, in the last third of the poem)

199 **the arms of the divine Achilles** a gift of the gods to Peleus at his marriage to Thetis (see Book 18, lines 84–5) and therefore presumably imperishable like the set of arms made for him, also in Book 18

376 **the fog** compare Book 15, line 668 and Book 16, line 567 where Zeus spreads night about the body of Sarpedon, thus adding to the confusion and danger. Compare also lines 366 and 644

426 **the horses of Achilles** compare Book 19, lines 404–17 where they speak

547 **a sombre rainbow** usually ominous in Homer (compare Book 11, line 27)

647 **Kill us in daylight, if you must** the final line of Aias's prayer is a famous one

BOOK 18 The making of the arms

Antilochus brings news of Patroclus's death to Achilles. Thetis hears Achilles's cries of despair and comes to him. He tells her that he will rejoin the fighting. She promises to bring him new armour at sunrise next day. Hector overtakes the Aiantes returning with the body of Patroclus. Iris warns Achilles and he frightens off the Trojans by appearing with the aegis which Athene has lent him. Night falls. Hector rejects Polydamas's advice to withdraw into the city. The Greeks grieve for Patroclus and wash his body. Thetis prevails upon Hephaestus to make new armour for her son. There is an elaborate description of the shield.

The calamitous death of Patroclus, whom he loves more than his own life (lines 81–2), becomes the calamity of Achilles. When the news reaches him, Achilles, in conversation with Thetis, fully recognises his own error and folly. The gods have done much for him but there is no pleasure in achievement any more. He is ready for death, regrets his special destiny as the son of a goddess and recognises the insidious effects of anger that can darken the wisest mind, is sweeter than honey and spreads like smoke. But the quarrel must be put behind him, and he yields to necessity, accepting the fate which Thetis has revealed to him. Even Heracles, the favourite of Zeus, was finally subdued by the anger of Here. Achilles resolves to seek glory and the death of Hector (lines 79–126).

By way of contrast to what has gone before, this book contains the most famous extended description in the poem featuring the shield made for Achilles (lines 478ff.) who needed new armour after Hector had despoiled the body of Patroclus. The pictures on the shield have no direct connection with the rest of the poem (though there is a besieged city), and are not from heroic myth or legend. They may be regarded as encapsulating the whole world, an eternal world of human activity transcending the Trojan War, for the sun, the moon and the stars are at its centre and the Stream of Ocean borders the shield (line 607) as in the Homeric view it borders the world. In the city at peace is a representation of a trial by jury, the beginnings of public justice and criminal law. Though many of the scenes are idyllic the overall picture is not idealised, for there is a city at war and even in the city at peace there has been a homicide.

What the poet admires in the shield is the realism of the pictures (the soldiers are said to drag off their dead like real living men) and the ability of the divine craftsman Hephaestus to make the most of his raw materials for highlighting purposes. The gods are larger than life and wrought in gold; the unploughed field is made of gold while behind the plough the soil is black as in real life (line 549). The vineyard is gold, the grapes are black, the ditches blue and the fences tin. The cows are of gold and tin. The use of metals of different kinds and colours and the art of inlaying bronze were well established in Mycenaean times.

The vigour of the divine craftsman setting about his task is matched by the vigorous descriptions of energetic activity in the pictures themselves. The final picture celebrates dancing and song, as the bard sings to the accompaniment of his lyre and the young men and women dance. The whole description is a discreet celebration of the divine power of art and of the artist as god.

38 **every Nereid** the daughters of Nereus, the old man of the sea. They are sea nymphs of the Mediterranean

203 **Athene cast her tasselled aegis round his sturdy shoulders** Achilles has the aegis: to inspire terror; he is the only mortal to be lent armour by a divinity

219 **as the trumpet** not used in Homeric battles

289 **the gold and bronze, of Priam's city** it is implied throughout the poem that Troy is a magnificent city, opulent and cultivated, so that the fall of Troy is the destruction of an ancient and cultivated civilisation

336 **I will cut the throats of a dozen of the highborn youths of Troy** this is carried out at Book 21, line 26

373 **three-legged tables** with wheels; examples of these, of Phoenician craftsmanship, are known to have existed

382 **Charis** this means 'grace'. The artificer needs grace to effect his art. In the *Odyssey* Hephaestus is married to Aphrodite

397 **a cripple** compare the story of his fall at Book 1, lines 590–4, where he is thrown out by Zeus. The Greeks did not have a liberal attitude to physical deformity. Crippled infants were generally left in the open to die of exposure

432 **marriage to man** Thetis married the mortal Peleus; there is a legend that Zeus knew that Thetis was destined to bear a son who was stronger than his father, and therefore made sure that she married a mortal

470 **the bellows** they work by command from the god

487 **Orion and the Bear** in Northern Greece when Orion rises, the Bear is on the horizon from which he immediately ascends. As he is about to bathe in the ocean, the Bear is frightened by the presence of Orion the giant hunter

570 **the lovely song of Linus** usually said to be a dirge for the death of the young Linus, perhaps a personification of the spring or the summer

592 **Daedalus** the word means 'cunningly wrought' and is the name given to the artisan employed by the Cretan king Minos at Cnossus. He built the labyrinth, a maze in which the Minotaur was imprisoned. Ariadne was the daughter of Minos who helped Theseus escape from the labyrinth by means of a thread after he had killed the monstrous Minotaur

BOOK 19 Achilles and Agamemnon are reconciled; Briseis is restored

Thetis brings the new armour to Achilles. Achilles summons an assembly and announces that he will end his feud with Agamemnon and return to the battlefield. Agamemnon publicly admits his folly and offers Achilles gifts and the return of Briseis. Achilles does not reject the offer but urges immediate engagement with the enemy. Odysseus insists upon feeding the troops first. The gifts and Briseis are brought forward. The troops eat, while Achilles abstains. Athene strengthens him with nectar. The Greeks assemble and Achilles arms. His horse Xanthus predicts his death.

Achilles now has a completely new perspective on things. The great quarrel is now simply 'a feud about a girl' (line 58). Briseis is again a mere chattel and spoil of war as she had been in the first book. In Book 9 Achilles says that he loves her with all his heart (Book 9, lines 342–3), and Thetis tells Hephaestus that he missed her greatly (Book 18, line 446). Here it is clear that whatever he felt for Briseis, he loved Patroclus with far deeper feeling. His death affects him more than would that of his father or his son (lines 321–7).

Although Agamemnon blames Ate (line 91), a personification of folly or rashness, this is simply the Greek way of admitting error; his apology is complete and abject, as evidenced by his repetition of the offer of gifts and the fact that it is given publicly before the army. When he briefly addresses the army, Achilles takes up the point that a man can be utterly blinded by Zeus (line 270) but the generalisation though it clearly refers to Agamemnon might also extend to himself. He does not indulge in any further reproaches. He is now focused only upon revenge and the death of Hector. His intensity is seen in his desire that the army should fight immediately and forgo food. Odysseus by contrast has a more sensible approach.

38 **red nectar** nectar is the wine of the gods, hence the adjective 'red'
87 **Fate** the Homeric word is Moira which means 'portion' or 'lot'
99 **Here** Here is the goddess of childbirth
123 **Eurystheus** not a son but a great-grandson of Zeus. His grandfather Perseus, who slew the Gorgon, was son of Zeus and Danae. Heracles performed his twelve labours at the command of Eurystheus
292 **Achilles' lawful wife** at Book 9, line 336 Achilles does call Briseis his wife. It seems strange that the son of a goddess should marry a captive
325 **wretched Helen** only here does any Greek speak ill of Helen
413 **the Son of Leto** Apollo (see Book 16, lines 788–93)
418 **the Furies struck him dumb** perhaps because the Furies overlook Destiny, and it is not the destiny of horses to speak

BOOK 20 Achilles returns to the fighting and the Gods join the battle

Zeus gives the gods permission to take sides in the war. Apollo in the guise of Lycaon urges Aeneas to confront Achilles. They meet and Aeneas is about to be killed when he is rescued by Poseidon. Achilles and Hector inspire their troops. Apollo warns Hector to avoid Achilles. Achilles kills numerous Trojans including Polydorus. Hector faces Achilles to avenge his brother. His spear-cast is deflected by Athene. Apollo snatches Hector away. Achilles continues the slaughter elsewhere.

Achilles is now at the forefront of the action and the narrative. In the council at the beginning Zeus allows the gods to join in to prevent Achilles from sweeping all before him. This has the effect of raising him in the audience's imagination. Both Aeneas at the beginning and Hector at the end have to be protected and rescued by the gods from his terrifying onslaught. The element of chivalry that was apparent in the earlier part of the poem is extinguished in its later stages. The abortive encounter with Hector who is rescued by Apollo artfully anticipates the poem's climax while postponing it and prolonging the tension.

7 **not a single River stayed away** it is not clear why all the river gods come to the council. In the next book the river god Scamander takes part in the fighting

8 **the Nymphs** freshwater nymphs are Naiads, wood nymphs are Dryads

30 **he may cheat Destiny** Achilles is destined to fall before Troy

53 **Callicolone** the name means 'beautiful hill'

92 **Lyrnessus and Pedasus** towns in the Troad sacked by the Greeks before the siege of Troy

145 **Heracles** Poseidon sent the sea beast to plague the Trojans because Laomedon (Priam's father and king of Troy) had cheated him and Apollo of their promised payment for building the walls of Troy (see Book 21, lines 436–60). Heracles saved Hesione, Laomedon's daughter, from the clutches of the monster. Heracles was evidently aided by Athene who was not hostile to Troy until the judgement of Paris which came later

203 **we know each other's parents** Aeneas then goes into great detail; compare the similar speech of Glaucus to Diomedes in Book 6

308 **his children's children in the time to come** Aeneas has a special destiny in Homer; he is to ensure the survival of the Dardan race. Later writers developed the story, notably the Roman poet Virgil (70–19BC) in the *Aeneid* in which Aeneas, after the sack of Troy and the death of Priam, leads the remnant of his people to Italy where his descendants found Rome

413 **Achilles too was quick on his feet** Achilles's recurring **epithet** 'swift of foot' is highly appropriate here

434 **better by far than myself** Hector is not thinking of morals, but of the warrior's prowess. Possibly there is **irony** here

BOOK 21 Achilles fights the river god Scamander

Achilles drives the Trojans to the river Scamander whose waters become choked with bodies. He kills Lycaon whom he had previously spared, and Asteropaeus, a descendant of a river god. As a descendant of Zeus, Achilles asserts the superiority of his ancestry. Scamander, already angry, rebukes Achilles and threatens to overwhelm him. In difficulties Achilles is rescued by Here who commands Hephaestus, the fire god, to check Scamander. The gods then war among themselves. Ares, Aphrodite and Apollo, the supporters of Troy, are discomfited. Achilles chases the Trojans to the city but is distracted by Apollo taking the form of the Trojan Agenor.

The darkening moral tone of the poem is marked by Achilles's determination (which he later acts upon, with the poet's disapproval, at Book 23, line 175) to sacrifice twelve young men as blood price for the dead Patroclus. His treatment of Lycaon whom he had previously spared reveals his implacable nature and offers a foretaste of what is to come for Hector. The episode, with the contrast of Achilles's earlier reprieve of Lycaon, is designed to show his new and utter ruthlessness in the wake of the death of Patroclus. 'Even Patroclus died, who was a better man than you by far' (line 107); this utterance comes from one of his most famous speeches, showing a ruthless fatalism.

The fight with the river god Scamander may be contrasted with that of Diomedes with Aphrodite, which was not without a comic dimension. But there is no comedy here. Achilles's arrogant challenge to the god goes quite beyond the behaviour of Diomedes and elevates him to the level of a natural force. Indeed the god says to him 'you are more than man' (line 214). His heroic spirit is manifest in his horror at the prospect of death by drowning, an ignominious end that brings no fame: he would rather have been killed by Hector (line 279). The mixture of men and gods in the subsequent fighting serves to accentuate the distinction between them and to highlight the seriousness of mortality.

41 **Jason's son** Euneus, king of Lemnos, an island in the Aegean sea. Jason was leader of the Argonauts who sailed in quest of the golden fleece

43 **Imbros** an island near Troy

Arisbe on the coast of the Hellespont

65 **to reach his knees** Thetis likewise touches the knees of Zeus in the manner of a Greek suppliant (Book 1, line 512)

76 **whose bread I broke** as if he had been a guest

85 **Laothoe** Priam had fifty sons and therefore a number of wives. None of the Greeks in the poem seems to have been polygamous

91 **Polydorus** he is killed at Book 20, lines 408–18

131 **sacrificing bulls** rivers are frequently personified as bulls in Greek art. Scamander roars like a bull at line 237

140 **Asteropaeus** he is related to a river, so that his death is an appropriate prelude to the fight with the river god

154 **Paeonia** in Thrace

194 **Achelous** a great river in Aetolia in north-western Greece

223 **Scamander** he teaches Achilles that a mortal, even a descendant of Zeus, is no match for a god. Diomedes had wounded Ares and Aphrodite with the help of Athene

464 **those wretched creatures who, like the leaves** compare Glaucus at Book 6, line 146. The gods who support Troy are well beaten in this scene, a portent of what is to come. Zeus is highly amused at the spectacle

526 **Priam ... saw the gigantic Achilles** Homer reintroduces Priam in preparation for the final scenes

BOOK 22 Achilles kills Hector

Hector, at the Scaean Gate, is entreated by Priam and Hecabe to enter the city. He determines to stand his ground, though when Achilles comes after him he flees and is chased around Troy three times. Zeus weighs their fates on his golden scales. Hector is doomed. Apollo deserts him; Athene comes to aid Achilles, taking the form of Deiphobus, Hector's brother, and induces Hector to face Achilles. In the fight Hector is killed, having predicted in his dying words the death of Achilles. Achilles, watched by Priam and Hecabe, ties Hector to his chariot and rides off dragging the body behind him. News reaches Andromache whose lamentation closes the book.

Sympathy is created for Hector by the regret of Zeus that he must die and by the part played in his death by the gods, notably Athene who takes the form of his brother Deiphobus. When he finally faces Achilles, Hector attempts to make the bargain with him that he had made with Aias earlier, that the body of the loser will be restored (line 256). In murderous mood, however, Achilles will have none of it; he wishes he could summon up the appetite to eat him raw. It might be recalled here that in the heat of battle Hector himself had wanted to drag off the corpse of Patroclus, cut his head off and give it to the dogs of Troy (Book 17, lines 126ff.) and that later Hecabe wishes to do to Achilles what he wishes to do to Hector. Nevertheless there can be no doubt that Achilles is the most implacable spirit in the poem. Whatever may be thought of them (and the poet clearly disapproves of Achilles's behaviour), these are moments of raw feeling generated by the heat and suffering of war. This background makes the later meeting of Priam and Achilles all the more remarkable.

29 **Orion's dog** Sirius which rises at the height of the Mediterranean summer, hence the phrase 'dog days'

46 **Lycaon and Polydorus** their deaths are related in earlier books

93 **as a mountain snake** it was thought that the snake derived its poison from eating poisonous herbs

100 **Polydamas** see his advice in Book 18, line 249, which Hector ignored. He now regrets this and admits his weakness

105 **I could not face my countrymen** compare Book 6, line 442, in Hector's speech to Andromache

161 **This was no ordinary race** a celebrated passage

169 **I grieve for Hector** Zeus grieves as he had grieved for Sarpedon at Book 16, lines 433–8. Athene's reply is similar to Here's at lines 441–3

209 **the golden scales** compare Book 8, line 69

219 **you and I are going to kill him** Athene helps Achilles as she had helped Diomedes in Book 5. Apollo helps to kill Patroclus, and Achilles will be killed by the arrows of Paris and Apollo. Mortal and immortal powers work hand in hand

359 **Paris and Apollo** Hector prophesies Achilles's death; compare the prophecy of Patroclus at Book 16, line 854. He predicts the anger of the gods

385 **shameful outrage** this is the poet's own judgement of Achilles's abuse of Hector's corpse

500 **Astyanax** the lot of the fatherless in a patriarchal society was indeed difficult. For the reader who knows of Astyanax's actual fate (to be thrown off the battlements of Troy) the passage is doubly **pathetic**. Homer makes no reference to this, but see Andromache's fear at Book 24, lines 734–6

BOOK 23 The Greeks bury Patroclus and hold funeral games in his honour

Achilles continues to grieve. The ghost of Patroclus appears to him requesting burial for his body, which is then burned on a great pyre with much ceremony. Funeral games, presided over by Achilles, are held in honour of Patroclus. There is a chariot race, a boxing match, wrestling, a foot-race, a combat with spears, discus-throwing, an archery contest, and finally spear-throwing. Prizes are awarded by Achilles to the successful competitors.

The appearance of the ghostly spirit of Patroclus (Homer's word is *psyche* at line 65) and his request for burial is a cause of **pathos** in itself but also makes clear the necessity for burial and in so doing highlights the central issue yet to be resolved. Achilles tries to embrace the spirit, but it disappears gibbering and vanishes like a puff of smoke. Here is the Homeric conception of the afterlife as a miserable existence in an insubstantial world.

The funeral games that follow show Achilles in a more relaxed mode, adjudicating in disputes and presiding over the ceremony. No longer the lone outsider, he is integrated into the social world.

46 **shorn my hair** a sign of grief; compare line 135. The Greeks are 'long-haired'

73 **the River** probably Styx

87 **homicide** exile was the usual penalty

142 **Spercheus** a river in Achilles's native Thessaly. The hair is probably associated with strength and here with survival. By cutting off the lock, Achilles accepts that he will not return home

168 **taking fat** for the practical purpose of ensuring that the corpse will burn

185 **Aphrodite kept them off** even the Greeks admire the marvellous beauty of Hector (Book 22, line 370); it is therefore appropriate that the goddess of beauty should preserve his body

206 **a sacrificial banquet** compare Book 1, lines 423–4

291 **breed of Tros** for their capture by Sthenelus, Diomedes's squire, see Book 5, lines 321–4

556 **He gave him a gracious answer** Achilles keeps the peace; there is a fine **irony** in his words and role here

560 **the cuirass I took from Asteropaeus** captured at Book 21, line 183

BOOK 24 Priam visits Achilles to seek the ransoming of Hector's body

Achilles continues to outrage the body of Hector, hauling the corpse three times around the funeral mound of Patroclus. The gods take offence, and Zeus sends Thetis to tell Achilles to desist and accept a ransom. Zeus then sends Iris to Priam to tell him to go to Achilles with a ransom for Hector. Hecabe tries to dissuade him, but Priam sets off in the night and is met by Hermes disguised as a young Myrmidon prince who escorts him to the Greek camp. Achilles is moved by Priam's appeal and accepts the ransom. He urges Priam to eat with him and prepares sleeping quarters for him. Priam asks for a truce for burial which Achilles grants. He is warned by Hermes to return before dawn in case the other Greek leaders find him. Hermes escorts him back to Troy. Lamentations by Andromache, Hecabe and Helen are followed by the burial of Hector.

> Priam and the god Hermes, disguised as a young Myrmidon, address each other as father and son, thus preparing us for the emotions of the actual meeting between the Trojan king and the Greek champion. That Priam should kiss the hand of the man who has killed so many of his sons is a most intense and remarkable moment, the drama of which is fully appreciated by the protagonists themselves. Priam appeals to Achilles by reminding him of his own father, the aged Peleus. In this patriarchal society, the bond between father and son is of central importance. In Achilles's gentle treatment of Priam there is true magnanimity. Achilles looks beyond his own grief and anger, and comes to a calm and steady recognition that men can do no more than bear the indiscriminate mixture of good and bad that comes from Zeus. In the examples of Peleus and Priam he sees the insecurity and incompleteness of human happiness; grief is of little use in the face of the inevitability of human suffering (lines 518–51). Struck by Priam's bravery and responding to his appeal, while Priam weeps for his son Hector, Achilles weeps for his father Peleus who, he knows, will be left without an heir and defender when he himself falls at Troy. The momentary flaring up of his anger when he feels that Priam is pressing him too far is a deft stroke of psychological realism on Homer's part. But Achilles collects himself, and he urges Priam to share a meal. The taking of food **symbolises** the practical acceptance of continuing life and the recognition that even the passion of grief must yield to necessity. Amid the ruins of human hope and in the knowledge of imminent death, Achilles for the first time sees life steadily and sees it whole.

28 **Paris** he was shepherding his flocks on the slopes of Mount Ida when he was asked to make his judgement

44 **Achilles, who has no decent feelings** Apollo uses a key Homeric word here: *aidos*, restraint

53 **He had better beware of our wrath** from the Greek verb used here comes the noun 'nemesis'

59 **Achilles is the son of a goddess** Here is hardly concerned with the moral issue, merely with Achilles's status

66 **the gods loved Hector too** Hector's piety is frequently remarked upon. Zeus's proposal for the ransom recognises that Achilles's honour must be protected. There must be gifts in exchange for the corpse. No mention of Priam is made to allow for the great astonishment felt by Achilles when Priam enters his tent

257 **Troilus** famous in later legend, this is the only mention of him in the poem

340 **the lovely sandals ... wand** Hermes's traditional attributes as guide and messenger. One of his functions was to escort the souls of the departed to Hades, so that he is closely associated with both sleep and death

527 **Zeus the Thunderer has two jars** a famous passage. Peleus and Priam experience a reversal of fortune, in Priam's case most thoroughly. Priam's realm extended well beyond the bounds of Troy, both inland and to neighbouring islands

544 **Macar** this means 'happy' in Greek

592 **Patroclus, do not be vexed with me** Achilles apologises to him for allowing Hector's body to go for burial. He had vowed not to permit this at Book 23, lines 182–3

602 **Niobe** she was turned into stone as a favour in answer to her own request. The gods rewarded her faithful grief. If Niobe took food, then so may Priam without the reproach that he lacks feeling

615 **Sipylus** in Lydia, in Asia Minor

PART THREE

CRITICAL APPROACHES

The commentaries following the book by book summaries have pointed to features of Homer's art in the management of the plot, the presentation of character, the handling of theme and the use of language. Such is the intensity and concentration of the present action of the poem that the reader may lose a sense of the overall direction of the plot. What follows here seeks to give an overall view.

THE WELL-MADE PLOT

UNITY OF ACTION

The *Iliad* does not give us the story of the Trojan War in a straightforward way, for it narrates neither its beginning nor its end; it begins in the middle of things or to be more accurate near the end of things, at a critical point in the proceedings in the ninth year of the siege. Nor is it an *Achilleid* based on the life and character of Achilles; indeed, the hero is absent from nearly two thirds of the action. Its main action has to do with the anger of Achilles; this is the source of its unity.

Slighted by Agamemnon in a quarrel, Achilles angrily withdraws from the fighting and asks his goddess mother Thetis to persuade Zeus to give the Trojans success so that the Greeks will be forced to recognise his worth (Book 1). Zeus acts upon his promise, and the leading Greeks are wounded (Book 11). With the Greeks in danger of defeat, his friend Patroclus persuades Achilles to allow him to fight wearing his armour. Patroclus is subsequently killed by Hector (Book 16). Stung by grief and remorse Achilles returns to the battle to avenge his friend. He kills Hector in single combat and drags off his corpse fixed to his chariot (Book 22). The dreadful consequences of his anger to himself and to others are shown in full. These four books (1, 11, 16, 22) contain the main action and what may be called the irreducible plot of the *Iliad*. There is a clearly discernible chain of cause and effect both in the actions of the gods (who accept the rulings of Fate) and in the actions and characters of men bringing about certain natural or probable consequences, leading inexorably to the death of Hector and the climax of the poem.

While there is a simple single action in the *Iliad*, the great art of the poet is apparent in the skill with which the main plot is expanded. The scope of the poem is immediately widened so that it is not confined to the anger of Achilles, but becomes truly an *Iliad*, that is a poem embracing the whole Trojan story (Ilium being another name for Troy). In Book 1 the request of Thetis that Zeus aid her son becomes the will of Zeus, and in the opening of Book 2 Zeus begins to act upon his promise by sending a false dream to Agamemnon. This has the effect of starting the fighting, but it does not immediately result in Trojan success. The first day's battle after the resumption of fighting in Book 2 is inconclusive and little happens to advance the plan until Zeus reasserts himself in Book 8. The main function of the first day's activity (Books 2–7) is twofold: the protagonists on both sides are introduced and the general context in which the main action takes place is revealed.

The expansion of the plot could have been accomplished by a retrospective narrative by one of the characters of events leading up to the present. In the *Odyssey*, Odysseus tells his past adventures to the King of the Phaeacians in an after-dinner speech (Books 9 to 12), but in the *Iliad* Homer fills in the past and broadens the scope of his poem without relinquishing his present narrative. In fact the past becomes a cause of dramatic interest in the present, in the duel between Paris and Menelaus for example. The past is incorporated indirectly into the present with no sacrifice of immediacy or dramatic tension. What is perhaps sacrificed is some measure of probability. Strictly speaking, it is improbable that the warring parties would agree to a duel to settle all after a nine-year siege. We may feel that Priam should be able to recognise his principal opponents, and that it might have occurred to the Greeks to protect their ships with a wall earlier in the campaign. Homer's method results too in incongruities. It has often been pointed out that the catalogue of ships is a more appropriate account of their assembly at Aulis where the Greeks had gathered to sail in the first place. But though the main action of the poem is entirely probable and satisfactorily linked together by a chain of cause and effect, the *Iliad* is not constructed like a nineteenth-century naturalistic novel. Homer's primary concern is the continuously unfolding drama of the immediate present.

The main action of the irreducible plot is first diversified and enriched by the various episodes in Books 2 to 7 which widen the scope of the poem to embrace the whole Trojan war. The second expansion of the irreducible plot is the skilful prolongation and retardation of the action in which Zeus carries out his plan to give the Trojans success so that the Greeks will appreciate the worth of Achilles. Book 11 contains all that is strictly necessary for this phase of the irreducible plot, but the action is prolonged from Book 8 to Book 15, principally by two simple devices. The will of Zeus is thwarted by the activities of other gods, and in the human sphere of military tactics the Trojan advance takes place by stages involving the capture of the central ground (Book 8), the breach of the wall (Book 12) and the arrival at the ships (Book 15). In the first day's fighting (Books 2–7) Zeus does not act decisively; he sends the dream to Agamemnon and instructs Athene to cause Pandarus to break the truce, but other actions of the gods influence the course of events, notably the support of Athene for Diomedes. In the second day's fighting (Book 8) Zeus decides to bring matters to a head and forbids the other Olympians to take part in the war. The Trojans have considerable success and are able to camp on the Trojan plain. This Greek reverse leads to the embassy to Achilles, and to the plan to reconnoitre the Trojan camp by night (Books 9 and 10). The course of the action is not directly affected by the embassy or by the night expedition, so that the third day's fighting continues where the second left off. Zeus allows Agamemnon some early reward but promises Hector success until sunset. The leading Greeks, Agamemnon, Odysseus and Diomedes, are then wounded, and Aias is forced to retire (Book 11). The action is prolonged in the next book by the fight at the wall which the Greeks have built to protect their ships (Book 12). In the next two books (13 and 14) the action slows down when Zeus later takes his eye off the fighting, thus enabling Poseidon to encourage the Greeks, and when he is lulled to sleep by Here. In Book 15 Zeus awakes and Trojan fortunes are restored, and some slight advance is made upon the state of events at the end of Book 12 in that the Trojans are not only through the wall but threaten the ships themselves. This brings us to the pivotal turn in the action with the deaths of Sarpedon and Patroclus in Book 16.

At this pivotal point two thirds of the way through the narrative, the poet has managed to expand and diversify the irreducible plot without losing sight of it, and without allowing any of the episodes to acquire undue significance. Because everything is narrated in the present tense, there is, generally speaking, the illusion of vigorous forward movement, but in reality most of what happens before Book 16 is inconclusive and inconsequential, in that the main action is not seriously affected. The flight of the army, the inconclusive duel between Menelaus and Paris, the truce made and broken, the ***aristeia*** of Diomedes that ends in an exchange of gifts, the inconclusive duel of Hector and Aias, the building of the wall that is later breached, even the embassy to Achilles, the night attack, the *aristeia* of Agamemnon that ends in his being wounded, the intervention of Poseidon, the *aristeia* of Idomeneus broken off because he is too weary to continue, the intervention of Here and the wounding of Hector – all these actions serve to extend and interrupt the main action, but no one of them is allowed significantly to develop to a point where it threatens to complicate the essential simplicity of the main action that constitutes the irreducible plot.

Furthermore, the narrative skill of the poet is apparent in the gradual build-up to the pivotal action of Book 16. The death of Sarpedon, which is to motivate Hector to pursue Patroclus, is the first death of significance, artistically speaking, in the *Iliad*. It is marked by unusual divine interest: Zeus actually contemplates suspending fate for the sake of his beloved son. In all the fighting prior to Book 16 there are no significant scenes of **pathos** involving a major hero, and Sarpedon is the first figure to be given a death speech of some length. The deaths of Sarpedon and Patroclus provide material of importance for repetition and variation in the later narrative of the death of Hector, but they do not simply offer repetition of what has gone before in the poem.

There is a gradual building up to the pivotal calamity, whence the poem moves much more directly to its climax. The irreducible plot could be expanded equally well after the pivotal turn as before, but there is no artistic reason for significant delay after the calamity. The proportions of two thirds before the pivotal calamity and one third following it is a satisfying structure, and reflects the stubborn persistence of Achilles's angry withdrawal, and the rapidity with which events take their necessary course after Achilles's return. From the death of Patroclus to the death of Hector and the close of the poem the narrative is carefully paced, with each stage contributing to the cumulative effect.

The struggle over Patroclus's body in Book 17 follows naturally from his death and dramatises the concern for the proper treatment of the dead, which is to be a major factor at the close of the poem when Achilles abuses Hector's corpse. The episode in which Hephaestus makes arms for Achilles (in Book 18) is well integrated into the main action since Nestor in Book 11 suggests to Patroclus that he fight in Achilles's armour. When Hector despoils Patroclus's corpse, Achilles is in need of a new set of armour now provided by the gods. The pause in the action here is natural, artistically and logically. The narrative of the third day's fighting has been continuous, stretching over seven books. This is an ideal moment for an interlude which takes us beyond the narrow focus of the fighting on the plain of Troy. In Book 19 comes Achilles's reconciliation with the Greeks, followed by preparations for the final day's fighting. In the argument over whether they should first take food, Odysseus points out that the meal is a practical necessity, but the taking and sharing of food, from which Achilles here abstains, is given a **symbolic** significance that will be apparent again in the final book when Achilles persuades Priam to eat. In Book 20, Achilles's ruthless fighting power is established. There is some slowing down which intensifies suspense when Hector, who faces Achilles when the latter kills his brother Polydorus, is whisked away by Poseidon. In Book 21, Achilles's power and stature are made more formidable in the fight with the river god. After the death of Hector in Book 22, the **episode** of the games in Book 23 is of course superfluous to the main action but it arises naturally from it, providing a release of tension and change of mood after the fighting of the previous day and before the solemn proceedings of the final book in which the anger is finally resolved.

The construction of the poem, therefore, however loose and elastic it may appear, is carefully plotted. The single simple action which gives the poem unity is expanded, prolonged and retarded, and paced with care to give maximum impact, first to the pivotal calamity and thereafter to the climax and its aftermath at the end. Everything expresses the one intention and contributes, in Aristotle's phrase, to one result, one end (*Poetics*, 23, lines 1–2).

UNITIES OF PLACE & TIME

Apart from essential **unity of action**, the *Iliad* also has unity of place: all the human action is concentrated in one small area embracing the Greek camp, the Trojan plain and the city itself. Finally, there is a remarkable concentration of time. The scale of the poem, its **episodic** nature and the apparently leisurely pace of the narrative are such that, **paradoxically**, it is possible to underestimate the tight and careful concentration of events into such a brief space of time. It may seem that Zeus has forgotten his promise, but in reality only one day passes before he takes vigorous action to carry it out, and only five days pass between the appeal of Thetis to Zeus in Book 1 and the death of Hector in Book 22. Allowing for a day's inactivity while both sides bury their dead, Achilles is absent from the fighting for just three days.

So concentrated is the *Iliad* that its whole action takes place in a mere fifty days. Of these twenty-two pass in Book 1. The plague rages for nine days and on the tenth Achilles calls a council. After the quarrel, Thetis promises to petition Zeus when the gods return after eleven days' feasting with the Ethiopians. A further twenty-two days pass in the last book. For eleven days Achilles regularly abuses the corpse of Hector. On the twelfth, the gods command him to desist. That night Priam comes to Achilles with a ransom. Achilles allows Priam a truce for the burial of Hector. The Trojans prepare for nine days and bury Hector on the tenth. The intervening events (from the end of the first book to the beginning of the last) take place in the course of six days.

After Achilles's withdrawal the first day's fighting takes us from Book 2 to the duel of Hector and Aias in Book 7. A day is then taken for the burial of the dead. On the next day Zeus acts vigorously on his promise to Thetis (Book 8). After the events of the night, described in Books 9–10, the longest section of the narrative covers the third day's fighting. Zeus promises Hector success until sunset. Hector kills Patroclus and, after the struggle over his body, news of his death is brought to Achilles (Books 11–18). The fourth day's fighting sees the return of Achilles and culminates in the death of Hector (Books 19–22).

On the following day Patroclus is buried (Book 23). Six days pass altogether, four days of fighting, two of burial.

The simple economy and clarity of design are apparent in the use made of intervening evenings and nights. Each is the occasion of some addition to the plot. Agamemnon's dream precedes the first day's fighting, and at the end of it councils take place in both camps, as well as negotiations for the burial of the dead. During the following evening and night the Greeks build the wall (Book 7). The next evening the embassy to Achilles occurs (Book 9), followed by the reconnoitre of the Trojan camp (Book 10). During the next night the Greeks mourn Patroclus, while Hephaestus makes new armour for Achilles (Book 18). After Hector's death, there is an evening council in the Greek camp and a meal. The ghost of Patroclus appears to Achilles (Book 23). Priam visits the tent of Achilles at night (Book 24).

This simple overall concentration of time and the overall unity of place are a consequence of the general poetic design, concentrating upon one single action. This action is diversified, extended and enriched by many episodes but the essential unity is not broken. The episodes do not extend the action to places far away from the plain of Troy, nor do they extend the temporal framework in which the main action takes place. Herein lies a simple source of the peculiar concentration and intensity of the *Iliad*. The main action of the irreducible plot of the *Iliad* in comparison to the subjects of other great **epics** is insignificant in itself. The essential subject of the *Odyssey*, the journey home, has grandeur of its own. In the *Aeneid* of the Roman poet Virgil, the essential subject is again a momentous one, of a journey and a struggle which are to make possible a great new civilisation. In *Paradise Lost* of John Milton (1608–74), the grand English epic constructed on classical principles, the subject is no less than the Fall of Man. Against these the anger of Achilles is in itself trivial, yet, paradoxically perhaps, no other epic has quite the scale of the *Iliad*, since scale is not something intrinsic to the subject of a poem, but is a consequence of the poet's concentrated presentation of that subject. Nobody can believe after experiencing the *Iliad* that the anger of Achilles is a trivial thing.

THE DIVINE MACHINERY & USE OF PROPHECY

There are two further features of the *Iliad* that contribute to the concentrated effect of the poem, adding both structural unity and scale. The first concerns the use made of the Olympian deities, the '**divine machinery**' of the poem. In the quarrelsome **episodes** on Olympus and in some of their interventions on the battlefield, Homer's anthropomorphic gods and goddesses diversify the main action by introducing comedy into the poem. In Book 1, after the seriousness of the quarrel between Agamemnon and Achilles, the quarrel between husband and wife on Olympus is presented in an altogether lighter vein. That the most powerful of the gods and their king should also be a hen-pecked husband is an amusing incongruity. At the same time the absurdities of the gods are sometimes a counterpoint to the seriousness of what happens in the mortal sphere; their inconsequential wounds and quarrels seem trivial in comparison to the serious wounds and quarrels of those who are subject to death. The intervention of the gods can also serve to magnify the significance of human actions. But whatever else may be said of the Homeric gods, they are a convenient structural device; hence the term 'divine machinery'.

The central action of the poem turns on the will of Zeus, on his promise to Thetis that the Trojans will succeed until the Greeks are forced to appreciate Achilles's worth. Every action is initiated by a god. Apollo sends the plague at the beginning of the poem. In the first day's fighting (Books 2–7) the various gods give their support to their favourites. On the second day (Book 8) Zeus acts more decisively on his promise and forbids the other gods to participate. In the third day's fighting (Books 11–17) Zeus promises Hector success until sunset. When he takes his eye off the fighting Poseidon intervenes and Zeus is then lulled to sleep by Here. On the fourth day after the return of Achilles (Books 19–22), the gods are allowed to take sides to make the contest more even for a while, until the gods supporting Troy are defeated by those encouraging the Greeks, and divine aid for Hector is withdrawn. Finally the close of the poem is brought about by the displeasure of Zeus who forbids Achilles to continue abusing Hector's corpse.

There is a further structural effect produced by the divine machinery. Greeks and Trojans have divine support in more or less equal proportions. Of the major divinities, Here, Athene and Poseidon support the Greeks while Apollo, Aphrodite and Ares support the Trojans. This has the effect of making a balanced structure. As the gods and goddesses have conflicting interests and purposes they can also be said to dramatise a view of the human condition in which humankind is a prey to conflicting amoral forces, for the ultimate Greek victory that is predicted does not come about because Zeus, the most powerful of the gods, wills it. He has nothing against Troy and the Trojans. This structure and vision is distinctively 'Iliadic'.

Related to this use of the divine machinery is the prophecy of future made by both gods and mortals. A prediction or foreboding has its particular local dramatic function, but the use of prophecy is also a means by which the poet reveals the structure of his poem and exerts his control over the narrative.

In the earlier part of the poem the prophecies are expressed in general terms. Thetis refers generally to the doom of Achilles when talking to her son (Book 1, lines 416–17). Agamemnon's instinct tells him that Troy will fall (Book 4, lines 163–5). In Book 6 the fate of Troy is identified with Hector, its chief defender. Andromache fears for her husband's safety, and Hector has the same prophetic instinct as Agamemnon (Book 6, lines 448–9), fearing for the city, its inhabitants, and chiefly for Andromache. The *Iliad* is narrated in the eternal present, but just as the past determines the structure of the present most obviously for Paris, Helen and Menelaus, so the future weighs heavily on the present for Achilles, Hector and Andromache. Just before the pivotal calamity, Zeus, who has not revealed the future so fully before, predicts not only the whole future course of the *Iliad* but also the future doom of Troy itself (Book 15, lines 59–77). Thereafter at crucial moments in the last eight books, Homer uses specific prophecy for dramatic effect. The narrator predicts Hector's doom at the moment when he puts on Achilles's helmet (Book 16, lines 799–80). In Hector's moment of triumph, the dying Patroclus predicts his death (Book 16, lines 852–4). Speaking to her son, Thetis confirms that his death will follow closely upon that of Hector (Book 18, lines 95–6). Achilles's death is further predicted by his horse Xanthus (Book 19, lines 409–10), by Achilles himself in reply (Book 19, line 421) and in more specific detail by the dying Hector (Book 22, lines 359–60). The future doom of the Trojans figures prominently in the pleas made by Priam and Hecabe to Hector just before the final combat, and also in the conversation between Priam and Achilles and in the lamentations with which the poem closes. Besides having **pathetic** or **ironic** effect at the moment of utterance, all these prophecies together propel the narrative towards its conclusion, while at the same time they suggest the workings of an inescapable destiny that is gradually being brought to pass through the apparently random chaos of present events.

Such is the scale of the poem that we may from time to time lose sight of the whole in the general flux of the fighting and miss the general direction of events. Decisive prophecies and divine interventions make the narrative outlines clear. If there were too few of them, the overall structure of events might not be clear, while if there were too many of them the sense of inevitable fate would be oppressive and would diminish the apparent freedom of the protagonists in the present action. Whether the inevitable fate is to be identified with the will of Zeus or whether the will of Zeus is simply an expression of a fate which binds gods and mortals alike matters little: when Zeus puts the fates of Hector and Achilles on the scales (Book 22, lines 209–13), the result is the same whatever interpretation is put upon the workings that bring it about. Such use of the divine machinery may be said to fulfil two related functions: in the first place, artistic cohesion is given to the poem, and in the second, the Greek sense of fate and its workings is given concrete and dramatic expression.

CHARACTER

AGAMEMNON

He is the leader of the Greeks by virtue of the fact that he has the largest contingent of ships. However, he is largely to blame for the quarrel, treating Achilles with a haughty disdain in depriving him of Briseis, his allotted spoil of war. His haughtiness is further shown in his rebukes to Odysseus (Book 4, lines 339ff.) and to Diomedes (Book 4, lines 370ff.).

He is rebuked for bad judgement and stupidity by Thersites (Book 2, lines 225–42), Odysseus (Book 4, lines 349–55), Diomedes (Book 9, lines 32–49) and Nestor (Book 9, lines 96–113). He admits his own folly (*ate*) privately before the Greek elders (Book 9, lines 115–16) and publicly before the army (Book 19, lines 72–144). In other respects he seems to be an irresolute leader. His trial of the army nearly results in the abandonment of the siege. Only the resourcefulness of Odysseus saves the day. When the Trojans reach the wall and the Greeks are wounded, he again suggests flight (Book 9, line 27) and has to be rebuked by Diomedes for his folly. When the Greeks have further reverses, he again suggests retreat and is roundly rebuked for defeatism by Odysseus (Book 14, lines 82ff.).

On the other hand he cuts an impressive figure in marshalling the army and despite the taunts of Achilles that he leaves the fighting to others, he distinguishes himself courageously in his ***aristeia*** (in Book 11), in which as king of men he is frequently compared to the lion, king of beasts. His kingly authority is reflected in the account of his sceptre made by Hephaestus for Zeus at Book 2, lines 101–8 and in the rich description of his armour at the beginning of his *aristeia* Book 11, lines 15–46.

ACHILLES

Achilles appears in Books 1, 9, 16 and 18–24 with a very brief appearance in Book 11. Like all Homer's characters Achilles is simply drawn. His nature as we see it in the *Iliad* is famously expressed by the Roman poet and critic Horace (65–8BC). If he is to be put upon the stage let him be:

> *impiger, iracundus, inexorabilis, acer*
> *iura neget sibi nata; nihil non arroget armis*
> (*Ars Poetica*, 12, lines 1–2)
>
> Impatient, quick to anger, ruthless, fierce
> Let him say laws are not made for him; let him put
> every question to the sword.

This is largely how we see Achilles after the quarrel scene in the opening book. Yet there are signs that before he became an angry man and became a figure always to be remembered for 'sulking in his tent', he was a figure of great magnanimity. He has a number of virtues. He was an only son and always speaks affectionately of his father, Peleus. He is closely bonded to his comrade-in-arms Patroclus with whom he wishes to share the glory of sacking Troy. Although even Patroclus becomes exasperated with him and tells him to his face that he is intractable (Book 16, line 29), he is not in fact a 'loner' who cannot deal with human relations. Moreover, he has acted chivalrously in the past in accordance with the high standards of the heroic code. Andromache recalls how when he sacked the city of Eëtion, he reverenced the dead, allowing decent burial of the enemy.

However, it is not as a character of exemplary virtues that Achilles excels. In fact he is not conspicuously good in any other sense than that he excels others in physical prowess (including running) and is the best fighter. This physical excellence (partly a consequence of his divine parentage) is the expression of a mighty spirit (*thumos*). But it is a dubious gift that both ennobles and reduces. Homer rarely comments on his characters directly. Either they comment upon each other, as when Helen characterises the leading Greeks to Priam (Book 3, lines 161–242) or they are characterised indirectly by their words and actions as in the case of Agamemnon, Nestor and Achilles in Book 1. But when late in the poem Achilles refuses mercy to one of his opponents in battle, Homer points out the futility of asking mercy from one who is not mild-spirited or of a gentle disposition but is *emmemaos*, impetuous or lost in passion (Book 20, lines 467–8). The Greek word here seems to be derived from the verb *mao* meaning to 'strive for', 'to yearn' or 'to desire greatly'. Certainly the passions and aspirations of Achilles, like those of other heroes, interlock and are inseparable. This close interrelation is emphasised in the **tragic** pattern of the *Iliad*.

Achilles, however, is not simply an aggressive and egotistical spirit over-prone to anger. His response to Agamemnon's insult is disproportionate to the offence but it has its origins in something magnanimous that is pure and noble. All the heroes share Achilles's heroic aspiration for glory but in none of them is it to be found in so intense a form. In Agamemnon it is tainted with the arrogance of power and the enjoyment of material possession; in Menelaus it is inseparably linked with the desire for revenge and recovery of what is his; in Diomedes it is restrained and moderated; in Odysseus and Nestor it is amenable to tactical and political considerations; in Aias it is largely unconscious to the extent that occasionally his brute strength is slightly comic; in Paris it is put aside for the sake of pleasure and in Hector it is complicated by the needs of those dependent upon him. Glaucus and Sarpedon fight partly to maintain their position among the Lycians. Only in Achilles is the aspiration pure and simple. He is not greatly interested in the Greek cause; he does not feel he has been wronged by the Trojans (Book 1, lines 152–60), and he is not fighting for hearth and home like the great patriot Hector who is his opponent. Achilles is bent upon heroic achievement for its own sake, not for what it brings with it in the way of material possessions, social position, a just revenge or the defence of loved ones. He fights simply and solely for glory. This purity of motive and aspiration is reflected in the choice he makes in remaining at Troy, preferring a short life with glory to a long life without fame (Book 9, lines 410–16). This choice itself is proof of magnanimity of spirit and there is nothing that the magnanimous Achilles would like better than to share his glory with his beloved comrade-in-arms Patroclus (Book 16, lines 97–100). With this purity of motive Achilles has an absolute sense of his own worth and of the honour due to him because of it. Any diminution of this honour diminishes the whole man, for honour is indivisible, and renders his choice of life null and void. There is honourable truth in this feeling, and Achilles honours this single truth so absolutely that he is blind to all other truths, so that his purity proves to be the ruin not only of many others but of himself too. His exceptional sense of personal honour springing from his single-minded and untainted aspiration to glory is at once the source of his greatness and of his great error. This **paradox** lies at the heart of Homer's tragic vision.

Finally it must be stressed that he is a character who undergoes a learning experience. To his great cost, he is wiser at the end than at the beginning. In the conversations with Priam he is not only restored to humanity but becomes the vehicle through which the poet expresses his tragic vision of the human condition.

Menelaus

As the wronged husband of Helen, for whose restoration the Greeks are fighting at Troy, he is a character in whom the audience have a special interest, even if in the plot of the *Iliad* he is overshadowed by his brother

Agamemnon. He has a major role in the fighting at the beginning where his duel with Paris in Book 3, watched by Helen from the walls, is the first fight involving the major heroes and he has the last ***aristeia*** in Book 17 before Achilles dominates the fighting at the end of the poem.

He is characterised as a man of few words (he has little to say in the poem) but is a good and honourable soldier; indeed one of his recurring **epithets** is 'dear to Ares' (the god of war). Another is 'of the loud war cry'; he is a guileless man of action. In the games at the end, he is angry with Antilochus for using dubious tactics to outsmart him in the chariot race. He is given no revealing speeches or reminiscences despite his centrality in the general story, nor do we have any glimpse into his feelings or the working of his mind. Nevertheless, in an exultant speech of triumph over the Trojan Peisanor (Book 13, lines 620ff.), he berates the Trojans for their excesses, predicting that Zeus the god of hospitality will make them pay for the abduction of Helen. In this, his only memorable speech, his words carry a special authority.

He easily gets the better of Paris in the duel but is prevented from killing him when Aphrodite whisks him away in a mist (Book 3, line 373). The truce made with the Trojans is broken when Pandarus treacherously shoots Menelaus with an arrow. Agamemnon is greatly concerned, but knowing it is a superficial graze, Menelaus does not make a fuss. When Hector proposes that the issue of the war be decided by a man-to-man fight, it is Menelaus who takes up the challenge, angrily accusing the rest of cowardice (Book 7, lines 96ff.). Knowing Hector to be the better man, Agamemnon orders him to hold back (line 110). Menelaus obeys without demur. He appears sporadically in the fighting thereafter but does not come into his own until he leads the fight for the body of Patroclus. Here the beginning of his exploits is marked by a notorious image: Athene implants in his breast the daring of a persistent blood-sucking fly (Book 17, lines 570ff.). He kills a Trojan but then Aias orders him to find Antilochus to tell Achilles of Patroclus's death. Menelaus obeys without demur. When he returns, he and Aias succeed in carrying away Patroclus's corpse. This is his one contribution to the plot. He is probably the least developed of the famous heroes.

AIAS

Like Menelaus, Aias is an uncomplicated soldier, though he is stronger than any other Greek except Achilles (see Book 2, line 768 and Book 17, line 279). In the duel with Hector in Book 7, he gets the better of the Trojan. As he advances to face Hector, he is likened in bulk and ferocity to Ares the war god himself and is described as 'bulwark of the Achaeans' (line 207). He and Odysseus lead the Greek resistance in Book 11 when they are under great pressure from Hector. He is a stout defender (forever associated with his sevenfold shield described at Book 7, lines 219ff.) and often seen in the thick of battle in reluctant retreat, notably in Book 11, lines 544ff. where he is likened in famous **similes** first to a cornered lion and then to a stubborn ass. He fearlessly confronts Hector on the rampage at Book 13, line 810 and fells him with a mighty stone at Book 14, line 409, forcing him to withdraw. With his brother Teucer, he confronts Hector again in Book 15, lines 415ff. where he rallies the troops against his onslaught. He cuts an impressive figure striding on the ships with a mighty spear at Book 15, lines 674ff. In Book 16, lines 102ff., there is a notable description of him being forced to retreat under pressure that leaves him painfully struggling for breath before his last encounter with Hector who forces him to retreat. It is at this point that Achilles sees the need to act and orders Patroclus to put on his armour and defend the ships. He is active in the fight to recover the body of Patroclus (Book 17, line 128), again forcing Hector to yield. Under pressure again in the long battle that follows and in virtual darkness as a result of a fog sent by Zeus, he utters a famous prayer to Zeus that, if he is to die, let it at least be in the daylight (line 629ff.). He and Menelaus manage to carry the body away.

He is part of the embassy sent to win over Achilles in Book 9. He speaks last when it is clear that Achilles will not yield. He bluntly accuses Achilles of letting down his comrades and persisting in stubborn pride. Achilles admits that his speech is almost after his own heart (line 645) as one soldier to another presumably. In the games he competes in the most physical encounter, the wrestling match, as well as the foot-race where he slips near the finishing post, ending up covered in dung, a comic moment appreciated by the spectators.

ODYSSEUS

Odysseus 'the much contriving' is the most subtle of the heroes, notable for his powers of persuasion. He saves the day when the troops stampede in flight after Agamemnon's trial of the army in Book 2. He chides and beats Thersites (Book 2, lines 246ff.) and encourages the army, reminding them of the prophecies of Calchas (Book 2, lines 284ff.). He is chosen to lead the embassy to Achilles in Book 9. He is taunted by Agamemnon (Book 4, lines 339ff.) and in turn accuses him of abject cowardice when he proposes flight (Book 14, lines 82ff.). He accompanies Diomedes on the spying mission in Book 10 to discover Trojan intentions. There is an extended description of his armour including the famous skull cap (lines 254ff.). He takes the lead in questioning the captured Dolon. After success in the fighting, he is wounded and rescued by Aias and Menelaus in Book 11, lines 439ff. Later against Achilles's wishes, he urges that the troops be fed before battle (Book 19, lines 155ff.) and advises Achilles to refresh himself. This advice Achilles rejects but he then offers advice showing similar common sense to Priam at the close. His part in the poem is not the greatest but he is a persistent presence, a reliable leader of sound understanding and a favourite of Athene who helps him withstand the power of Aias in the wrestling match where strength is checked by guile (Book 23, lines 725ff.).

DIOMEDES

Diomedes 'of the loud war-cry' is the youngest of the great heroes (Book 14, line 112). He plays a prominent role in the poem until he is wounded by an arrow from Paris at Book 11, lines 369ff. His behaviour is marked by a notable restraint. When he is rebuked by Agamemnon for holding back from battle in Book 4, lines 370ff. and compared unfavourably with his father Tydeus, a hero of the previous generation, he holds his tongue in respect for the king (line 402), in marked contrast to Odysseus before him and Achilles. His eventual rebuke of Agamemnon is therefore all the more telling. He starts with the assertion that criticism in council is lawful and reminds the king of his earlier rebuke before accusing him of faintheartedness in his desire to return home. After the failure of the embassy, he tells the king that it would have been better not to attempt it as it has made a proud spirit even prouder (Book 9, lines 697ff.). He urges that the fight be continued despite the wounds they have received at Book 14, line 128.

He proves his worth in his ***aristeia*** in Book 5, when in the first general battle of the poem he kills Pandarus (lines 286ff.), the breaker of the truce, who had previously wounded him in the shoulder with an arrow. With Athene's support he fights against the gods and even wounds first Aphrodite (lines 330ff.) when she intervenes to rescue her son Aeneas whom Diomedes has wounded, then later Ares, the war god himself (lines 855ff.). Unlike Patroclus later in the poem, he does not overreach himself and in his fight against the gods, unlike Achilles later, he does not exceed his powers and get into difficulties as a result. He volunteers for the spying mission in Book 10, chooses Odysseus as his companion and kills Dolon (lines 455ff.). Diomedes 'the tamer of horses' wins the chariot race in the games.

NESTOR

In the opening scene wise old Nestor who has seen it all before tries to calm the quarrelling heroes of a younger generation. He can see both sides and diplomatically urges compromise. He tries to cool the situation by speaking of his own exploits when he fought with Theseus in time past. He acts very much in this character throughout the poem. He helps to stiffen Agamemnon's resolve after the disastrous trial of the army and later offers him tactical advice (Book 4, lines 303ff.). He warns the soldiers not to waste valuable time looting (Book 6, lines 87ff.). He always speaks with authority and is heeded. He upbraids the Greek heroes with stories of past heroism when they are slow to respond to Hector's challenge (Book 7, line 123), takes charge of the casting of the lots for the duel (Book 7, line 170) and after it proposes burial of the dead and then the building of a defensive wall around the ships (Book 7, lines 325ff.). Though well past his prime, he joins in the fighting but has to be rescued by Diomedes (Book 8, lines 80ff.). He offers the best advice when the Greeks are in dire straits, urging Agamemnon to restore Briseis to Achilles (upbraiding him for not having taken his advice in the first place) and to placate him with further gifts (Book 9, lines 94ff.). He is instrumental in rousing the Greeks to a plan when Achilles refuses to co-operate and is the first to suggest the night mission to gather intelligence (Book 10, lines 204ff.). When in the following day's fighting, Achilles sees Nestor active in a rescue, he sends Patroclus to enquire the identity of the man rescued. He enters as the old man is about to take a meal and wine. Nestor's cup and the preparation of Pramnian wine are described (Book 11, lines 628ff.). Nestor then tells Patroclus of the further reverses of the Greeks, wishing he was young enough to do something about it. This occasions his longest reminiscence of past exploits (lines 668–761) after which he reminds Patroclus of the time when he (Nestor) and Odysseus were recruiting Achilles in Phthia. Peleus advised Achilles always to excel (line 784) while Menoetius, the father of Patroclus, told his son that as he was older than Achilles he should offer him advice. Nestor then urges Patroclus to persuade Achilles to let him fight with the Myrmidons wearing his armour (lines 796ff.) in the hope that the Trojans may mistake Patroclus for Achilles and desist, giving the Greeks a breathing space. Nestor's suggestion therefore initiates the action which is the pivotal turning point of the plot.

One of the **formulae** used of him is the phrase 'bulwark of the Achaeans'. When the Greeks are in dire straits, he offers a prayer to Zeus which evokes a response (Book 15, lines 372ff.) and a famous exhortation to the soldiers to be men and stand firm (Book 15, lines 661ff.). Another of his **epithets** is 'horseman' and more than once he is pictured driving his horses. It is fitting therefore that, in the games, he should be seen giving tactical advice to his son Antilochus for the horse race (Book 23, lines 306ff.). Antilochus, with inferior horses, uses the cunning advocated by Nestor and beats Menelaus into third place. Achilles honours Nestor with a prize in memory of Patroclus even though he was too old to compete in the games (line 620). Nestor therefore departs from the poem with a singular honour.

PATROCLUS

The close companion of Achilles: his death is the pivotal action of the poem and causes Achilles to return to the fighting to avenge the death of his friend. He had spent his youth in the house of Peleus and accompanied Achilles to the war (see above under Nestor). Though abstaining from the fighting with Achilles, on returning from Nestor's tent he has direct experience of the plight of the Greeks and attends the wounded Eurypylus (Book 11, lines 790ff.). In his ***aristeia***, he slays Sarpedon in a prolonged encounter and then is himself slain when he pursues Hector. He is first struck by Apollo (Book 16, lines 791ff.), then wounded by Euphorbus (lines 806ff.) before encountering Hector. In his death speech he predicts Hector's death at the hands of Achilles. The prolonged struggle over his body, the appearance of his spirit to Achilles, his burial and the funeral games in his honour all keep him in the audience's mind and testify to the centrality of his role in the poem and of the bond of friendship between comrades that the poem honours.

HECTOR

The great patriot and the mainstay of the Trojan resistance, he is at the forefront of the action of the poem throughout and his greater chivalry is a foil to the ferocity which causes Achilles to violate the heroic code. He is seen in domestic situations with his family and parents which has the effect of giving him an attractive human dimension so that some readers have thought that he is the true hero of the poem. Although he shares absolutely the heroic aspiration for fame and glory, he is also fighting for his loved ones and for his country so that his motivation is perhaps more easily understood than that of Achilles. He particularly dominates the action as a fiery fighting force between Books 11 and 16 when he leads the Trojan advance across the plain, breaks through the Greek defensive wall, threatens to fire the ships and kills Patroclus in the pivotal action of the poem. Thereafter he is sought with frightening intensity by Achilles; his death is the climax of the poem and its aftermath provides the resolution.

His challenge to the Greeks in Book 7, lines 67ff. is cast in noble language. The duel with Aias that follows is a much more thrilling contest than that between Paris and Menelaus that preceded it. Hector gets the worst of it, but as night falls heralds from both sides intervene to stop it. The magnanimous Hector proposes that they exchange gifts and part in friendship. His near defeat at the hands of Aias, the second best fighter of the Greeks, foreshadows his eventual defeat at the hands of Achilles who is the stronger fighter. The narrative of his final combat creates great sympathy for him as he experiences fear in the initial stages and is then deceived by Athene disguised as his brother. When he recognises that his time has come, he is resolute and stands firm, trying to repeat the chivalrous compact he had earlier made with Aias relating to the body of the slain. The ruthlessness of his opponent who compares himself to a wild animal (Book 22, line 262) puts his greater humanity into bold relief. His only compensation is that in his dying words he predicts the death of Achilles (lines 358ff.).

PRIAM

Although he is the king of a great city with many possessions, there is no trace in him of the arrogance of power. In fact, though a respected figure, he has little political role. In the Trojan council when Paris refuses Antenor's proposal that Helen be restored, Priam says nothing about this but goes on to propose a mutual burying of the dead (Book 7, lines 368ff.). An aged man, he appears as a tender father and is addressed as such even by Helen (Book 3, line 172) to whom he is courteous and gracious. When he appeals to Hector not to go out to face Achilles, he is a figure of pity, who laments the death of many of his sons at the hands of Achilles and who foresees further misery afflicting his household before an ignominious death for himself, mangled and eaten by the very dogs he has fed from his table. Achilles sees his own father Peleus and King Priam as piteous examples of the instability of human fortune. As a result of the *Iliad*, this is what Priam has become.

PARIS

Paris has a central role in the whole Trojan saga. When asked to judge which of the three senior goddesses, Here, Athene and Aphrodite was the most beautiful, he chose Aphrodite who had offered him Helen, the most beautiful woman in the world, thus alienating Here and Athene from the city of Troy. His abduction of Helen from Sparta is the direct cause of the Trojan War. There is a brief allusion to his judgement at Book 24, line 29 and Menelaus refers also briefly to the abduction of Helen (Book 13, line 626), but this is all in the past and, like Menelaus, he does not have a central role in the events of the *Iliad*. Nevertheless, he is a character in whom the audience will have a special interest. He is a foil to his brother Hector with whom he has an uneasy relationship. On his first appearance, he is rebuked by Hector as the curse of his father, his family and his city when, after issuing a challenge to the Greeks, he quails before an advancing Menelaus. 'And now are you too cowardly to stand up to the brave man you wronged? You would soon find out the kind of fighter he is whose lovely wife you stole. Your lyre would not help you at all, nor Aphrodite's gifts, those locks of yours and your good looks, when he had made you bite the dust' (Book 3, lines 52–5). In reply Paris admits that Hector's reproaches are fair but bids him not to scorn the gifts of Aphrodite. He agrees to the duel to settle the issue and is easily overcome by Menelaus but rescued by Aphrodite who whisks him off the battlefield and deposits him in his bedchamber to which she summons Helen and where they then make love. He is hated by the Trojans (Book 3, line 454) and again rebuked by Hector (Book 6, line 326). Nevertheless, he eventually rejoins the battle joyfully like a stallion released from the stable (lines 506ff.). In the Trojan assembly when Antenor proposes that Helen be restored, Paris refuses, though he offers to return all the treasure he took with her (Book 7, lines 357ff.). The Trojans, including Priam who speaks after him, make no attempt to change his mind.

In the subsequent fighting when he appears he always uses the bow, which is regarded as less heroic than fighting with spear and sword. In his death speech, Hector foretells that Achilles will be killed by Paris and Apollo (Book 22, line 359). Apollo is an archer and later literature tells how Paris killed Achilles by aiming an arrow at his heel.

HELEN

Helen, the ostensible cause of the continued siege, is introduced early on in the first Trojan scene. Iris, the messenger of the gods, visits her chamber where she is weaving battle scenes involving Greeks and Trojans on a tapestry and summons her to watch the duel between her current and former husbands. She sheds tears as she makes her way to the walls. Once there she is observed by the old men of Troy who give a famous testimony to her beauty: 'Who on earth,' they ask one another, 'could blame the Trojans and Achaean men-at-arms for suffering so long for such a woman's sake? Indeed she is the very image of an immortal goddess. All the same, and lovely as she is, let her sail home and not stay here to vex us and our children after us' (Book 3, lines 156–60). Nevertheless Priam addresses her affectionately and tells her that he does not blame her for the war but puts it down to the gods. In her respectful reply she adds, 'I wish that I had chosen to die in misery before I came here with your son' (line 173). She then identifies the Greek heroes for Priam, starting with Agamemnon: 'my brother-in-law once, shameless creature that I am' (line 180). Her first words here show a heavy consciousness of guilt.

After Aphrodite has rescued Paris, she goes to Helen in the guise of an old woman to summon her to his chamber. Recognising the goddess, Helen rebukes her and says she will not incur the anger of the Trojan women by sharing Paris's bed again. When the angry goddess threatens her, she submits. Her speech to Paris (lines 428–36) shows some confusion. At first she wishes he had died in the fight. Then she rebukes him for previously boasting that he was a better fighter than Menelaus, bidding him issue another challenge. But then she asks him for her sake not to war further with Menelaus in case he comes to grief. She follows Paris to bed.

When later Hector finds Paris with Helen in his chamber as he seeks him out to summon him to battle, Helen is abject in her self-reproach and expression of guilt: 'I am indeed a shameless, evil-minded and abominable creature' (Book 6, line 344). She wishes she had died at birth. Since the gods ordained otherwise, she wishes she had a better man for a husband, 'one with some feeling for the reproaches and contempt of his fellow men. But as it is, this husband I have got is an inconstant creature; and he will never change' (lines 351–3). She completes the lamentation of the women for Hector at the end of the poem, again wishing she had died before she came to Troy and recalling how Hector, like Priam, had always been gentle to her and protected her from the slights of others. As Homer presents her, she is an unhappy, sensitive and self reproaching victim, a figure of suffering caught in an unenviable position.

Andromache & Hecabe

The presence in the poem of Andromache, the gentle wife of Hector and mother of the infant Astyanax, and Hecabe, wife of Priam and Hector's mother, brings a poignant and humanising perspective to bear to the depiction of the masculine world of the warring heroes. Andromache's plea to Hector to remain inside the walls (Book 6, lines 407–39) is not simply used to elicit an heroic resolve on the part of Hector who must reject such a plea, but is both a heartfelt expression of love and a sympathetic representation not of feminine weakness but of the emotional cost of heroism to those who cannot partake of it, and perhaps to those who can. She is individualised but through her expressions of total dependence upon her husband and his fears for her if Troy falls when she will be sold into slavery, we see a stark representation of the evil consequences that await the defeated. She is for ever fixed in the world's imagination as a **symbol** of innocent suffering and a victim of the horrors of war. When Hecabe tries to dissuade Hector from going out to meet Achilles, she bears her breast in an archetypal gesture. She is here and in the final lamentation that she leads representative of mothers the world over bereaved of their sons. With the women's moving laments for Hector and with Andromache's foreboding for the fate of their infant son and her own life as an exile and slave (Book 24, lines 725–45), the poem ends not with a victory celebration for the conqueror but with a powerful evocation on the part of 'many-minded' Homer of the suffering that awaits all the innocent victims of war.

Heroic values

Homeric man seeks to make the most of his present existence in the material world. Few poems have so celebrated the vitality of immediate physical life and 'the body's fervour'. In a poem in which the world is at war it is to be expected that human worth should be reckoned by the standards of the warrior. In the quarrel old Nestor reminds Agamemnon and Achilles that he has known very much better men than they are, and it is clear that he means that the heroes of old were capable of greater physical prowess (Book 1, lines 256–66). Achilles owes his stature among the Greeks at Troy to the achievements of his own right arm and his swiftness of foot. When he rejects the pleas of Lycaon for mercy, he reminds Lycaon that Patroclus has died, who was a better man than he by far. Death will come even to Achilles who is beautiful and mighty and born of a goddess (Book 21, lines 107–13). Achilles measures his own worth here in strictly physical terms. Hector admits the superiority of Achilles (Book 20, line 434) and in the final confrontation Achilles tells Hector to stand his ground and prove his worth as a soldier (Book 22, lines 268–9).

When the heroes are propelled into action, what usually motivates them is a feeling in the blood, *thumos*. Many of Homer's words do not bear very exact resemblances to the English words used to translate them. *Thumos*, which seems to be related to the Greek verb meaning 'to rush along', is what causes strong feeling or passion. It is associated with natural strength, the heart, desire and appetite for food. It has to do with man's basic inner nature which for Homer is physical. To Andromache's plea that he refrain from fighting, Hector says that he would feel shame before the Trojan women if he did not join battle. But he also says that his *thumos* compels him to fight (Book 6, lines 441–6). However terrible the consequences, the heroes experience compulsion from within, so that the battles are whole-hearted and there is exhilaration in the fighting. Homer uses the word *charma* to express eagerness for battle and joy in the fight. When Apollo breathes *menos*, strength, into Hector, the Trojan leader is likened to a stallion who has broken loose and is galloping off joyfully to his favourite pastures confident in his own splendour (Book 15, lines 263–8). As he directs the fight, Zeus similarly glories in his own strength and power.

It is not only in the fighting that we are conscious of the physical world in Homer. There is much eating and drinking and talk of the feast amongst men and gods. For the gods life is an eternal banquet. Thetis tells Achilles that the gods are away in Ethiopia feasting and will not be back for twelve days (Book 1, lines 423–5). When the Greeks restore Chryseis, a sacrifice and a merry meal are described in detail (Book 1, lines 457–74). At the end of Book 1, Hephaestus reminds Zeus and Here that their quarrelling over the foolish race of man threatens to spoil their pleasure in the feast (lines 573–9). The gods are reconciled and drink to their heart's content. After the first day's fighting there is a meal in the

Greek camp at which Aias is rewarded with the best portion of beef (Book 7, lines 313–20).

The Homeric hero consciously endeavours to excel. Speaking to Diomedes, the Lycian Glaucus tells him that his father sent him to Troy with the advice always to excel over the rest and not to shame his forebears who were the best in Lycia (Book 6, lines 208–10). Nestor later tells Patroclus that when he had recruited Achilles for the Trojan expedition, the latter's father, Peleus, had told his son always to strive to outdo the others (Book 11, line 784). Hector's hope for his son Astyanax is that in future time men will say 'He is better than his father' as he returns from the battlefield bearing the bloodstained armour of his foe (Book 6, lines 479–81). The supreme test for the Homeric hero is, of course, the battlefield: this is where he will prove his excellence. But the desire to excel and the emphasis upon excellence are apparent throughout the poem, for instance, in the competitive spirit of the games in Book 23 where the competition for glittering prizes is as intense as it is on the battlefield, even if the stakes are not so high (compare Book 22, lines 157–61).

The promptings of the heroic spirit are most clearly articulated in the famous speech of Sarpedon at Book 12, lines 310–28. Sarpedon asks Glaucus why they are singled out for honour at the feast with special seats and the best food and drink among the Lycians who look upon them as gods. Why do they have the best land with orchards and wheatfields? Their social position obliges them to lead the Lycians in fighting so that their followers will acknowledge that they earn their privileges by virtue of their great prowess on the battlefield. At the same time Sarpedon says that if they could actually be like gods and avoid old age and death he would not urge Glaucus to join the fight where glory is gained. The Homeric adjective 'bringing glory' fits the context well. Elsewhere Homer uses many adjectives that express the grisliness of the fight. But since they cannot escape death in its countless forms, Sarpedon urges that they join the fight and either gain honour for themselves or give it to others. The heroic resolve is the conscious choice to risk a glorious death rather than to forgo glory for the sake of holding on to an insignificant life (compare the choice of Achilles at Book 9, lines 410–16).

The heroes of the *Iliad* therefore live what is on their terms a fully heroic life. There is consciousness of an heroic past in the nostalgia of the old soldier Nestor for past campaigns (see, for example, Book 11, lines 670–762) and in Agamemnon's account of the great expedition of the previous generation of heroes against Thebes (Book 4, lines 372–99). But the heroes of the present campaign are conscious of their own worth and fully confident of their superior strength. To Agamemnon's taunt that Diomedes is not so good a fighter as his father Tydeus, Sthenelus, Diomedes's squire, confidently asserts that the present generation of fighters are better than their fathers by far (Book 4, lines 404–10). The *Odyssey* by contrast is set in a post-heroic world: all the heroes of the Trojan War look back with nostalgia to an heroic past from the standpoint of a meaner domestic present.

In this intensely competitive world, possessions, prizes and gifts are valued in themselves but also for the distinction and honour they convey. This is also true of spoils taken from a defeated foe. It is because material possessions and prizes are a sign of the esteem in which the possessor is regarded that Achilles is so angered when Agamemnon takes his prize in the opening quarrel. Although Achilles later claims to love Briseis (Book 9, lines 342–3), in the quarrel itself and when the quarrel is mended, Briseis is regarded as a mere chattel (Book 1, line 185). In depriving Achilles of her, Agamemnon dishonours him and threatens the whole basis upon which relations are constructed in the Homeric world. Honour, pride, status and self-esteem (all that is contained in the Greek word *time*) are determining factors in relations between men, between gods, and between men and gods. Apollo's honour is affected when Agamemnon dishonours his priest. When Thetis appeals to Zeus to aid her son, she says that she will be the least honoured of the Olympians if he denies her request (Book 1, line 516). In many instances (for example, Book 9, lines 533–7) mortals incur the wrath of gods because sacrifices have been neglected. Conversely Zeus feels well disposed towards the Trojans and Hector because they have been generous in their offerings to him (Books 4, lines 43–9; Book 22, lines 168–72; Book 24, lines 66–70). Excellence must have due recognition and honour. The honour of the gods is respected when proper sacrifices are made; the honour of men is evident in material possessions.

Despite the compelling desire to excel and the intense regard that the Homeric hero has for his honour and self-esteem, the heroes are not an unscrupulous breed of supermen who have no regard for right and wrong and no sense of decency and **decorum**. In fact the contrary is the case. The converse of the great sense of honour felt by the heroes is the sense of shame expressed by Hector in Book 6. The Homeric word *aidos* is the restraining influence that on the one hand prevents cowardice and on the other prevents the concern for honour growing into overweening pride and arrogance. Included in the concept of *aidos* is reverence due to the gods, to elders and to the dead.

Implied in the Homeric word *themis* are codes of conduct that have been sanctioned by tradition. As the most powerful king, Agamemnon is privileged to test the army (Book 2, line 73) but custom allows Nestor to speak up against his folly (Book 2, lines 337–68). In the council in Book 9, Diomedes uses the privilege of freedom of speech in open council to criticise Agamemnon severely (Book 9, lines 32–49). The constitution of the Greeks at Troy is of course not democratic, but it is not difficult to trace here the beginnings of the Greek democratic spirit.

In their general manners the heroes observe the rules of orderly and civilised social behaviour. In the ritual of the meal and the sacrifice, there is a regular regard for proprieties. The **formulaic** character of the verse, in which there is repetition of customary actions, gives a strong impression of an orderly world of shared values and respect for tradition. The heroes habitually address each other with politeness and restraint. Even the gods address favoured mortals in a seemly manner. Priam is treated with exquisite tact by Hermes in disguise (Book 24, lines 331–447). Women (including Helen) are treated with attention, consideration and respect. In Homer they enjoy more freedom in their relations with men than seems to have been the case in later Greek history. When they discover that they are hereditary guest friends, Glaucus and Diomedes refrain from fighting and exchange gifts (Book 6, lines 212–35). Even under the stress of war the civilised decencies of the heroic world are generally maintained.

Excesses in the poem stand out against a background of moderate behaviour. Achilles's refusal to eat before the fight is in marked contrast to the good sense of Odysseus (Book 19, lines 216–37), and also to the advice he himself gives to Priam (Book 24, lines 559–620). Achilles's abuse of Hector's corpse contrasts with the civilised way in which he treats the dead of Andromache's family. The most obvious barbarities in the *Iliad* stand condemned by standards of civilised behaviour that are the norm in the heroic world.

THE *ILIAD* AS A TRAGEDY

Plato called Homer 'the first of tragedians' (*Republic* 606e) and in later Greek culture it became a commonplace that he was the father of **tragedy**. Aristotle in his *Poetics*, though he uses Homer as his touchstone when he is describing the desirability of unity in a work of art, is preoccupied there with drama. Nevertheless, the essential elements that he identified as prerequisites for the best sort of dramatic tragedy can first be seen in the plot and design of the *Iliad*. The fall from greatness that is one of the leading ideas associated with the tragic protagonist in Aristotle's analysis is not obviously charted in the *Iliad*, since the poem opens with the anger which is to distort Achilles's magnanimity. But centred as it is on the anger of Achilles, the poem does have the classic Aristotelian pattern of error (***hamartia***) leading to calamity (***pathos***) resulting in **ironic** reversal (***peripeteia***) which in turn brings about recognition of error and new awareness (***anagnorisis***).

The initial error in the quarrel scene may be regarded as originating with Agamemnon but when Achilles persists in his anger after the king has offered gifts in recompense in Book 9, the balance of error tips against him (as suggested above in the character analysis and in Extended Commentaries, Text 1). His continued abstention from the battle leads to his decision to allow Patroclus to aid the Greeks by fighting in his place, wearing his armour, in Book 16. This leads to the calamity of his death which results in unforeseen consequences. The calamitous death of Patroclus becomes the calamity of Achilles. He then recognises his error and undergoes a gradual revaluation. Honour and glory now have little meaning; in conversation with his mother Thetis he fully recognises his own error and folly. He is ready for death, regrets his special destiny as the son of a goddess and recognises the insidious effects of anger that can darken the wisest mind (Book 18, lines 79–126). In the ensuing fight his purity of motive (see Character, on Achilles) is now tainted with the desire for revenge, resulting in savage behaviour that makes him betray heroic ideals. At the end comes the second and fullest recognition scene:

in the meeting with Priam he comes to see suffering as the universal condition (Book 24, lines 518–51).

Homer gives us enough detail about Achilles to enable us to imagine a different treatment of his story. Zeus has allowed Thetis to produce a child who will excel all heroes (Book 18, lines 436–7). But Thetis tells Achilles that Destiny has given him a choice. If he stays at Troy he can win undying fame, but must himself die there; if he goes back home he can have a long life without glory (Book 9, lines 410–16). No reason is given as to why Achilles should have to make this choice; it has the arbitrariness typical of Greek myth. But in its pristine form, we can imagine that the myth was first and foremost an heroic myth, in which Achilles consciously makes an heroic choice in the full knowledge of its ultimate cost. Achilles is of course a supreme hero in the Homeric world, but Homer has developed the tragic possibilities latent in the myth. The heroic choice is taken for granted and is of secondary significance. The centre of Homer's action is the defeat of heroic expectation through folly and passion. Achilles is not a hero in control of his destiny but the victim of the arbitrary power of another man's folly and the imperious demands of his own nature. What happens to him in the poem is determined not by any external decree of the gods but by his own absolute sense of his personal honour. The climax of the poem is not the full-hearted celebration of heroic achievement but an act in which the glory of the hero is clearly tarnished (see Extended Commentaries, Text 3). The knowledge in which the greater humanity of the hero is revealed is not the confident knowledge of what his own heroic choice has cost him, but a bitter recognition of his own error and then an acceptance of necessary suffering as the universal condition, which quite transcends the original heroic myth. The tragic pattern imposed by Homer upon the heroic myth reveals a depth of humanity beyond the heroism of the hero, and the experience that the hero undergoes is the main burden of the poem's meaning and significance.

The general character of Homer's **oral formulaic** style and the mixture of dialects constituting Homeric language are described in The Language of Homer in Background.

Homer has always been praised by those who can read Greek for his great metrical harmony and the beauty of his poetry. Metrical harmony is obviously something that cannot even be suggested by a translation in modern prose. To read poetry in a prose translation is to be at some disadvantage. Nevertheless, if style is understood in its broadest sense, the beauty of Homer's style can be glimpsed even through Rieu's prose. For the beauty of the way something is represented cannot be wholly divorced from what is being represented. The beauty of Homer's conceptions and representations can be felt in any version.

The emphasis on excellence that has been noted in the previous section on Heroic Values affects everything that is represented in Homer and can be felt in his general conception of the world. Homer celebrates physical beauty in persons and material objects. In the descriptions of people there are many details, usually in the comments of others, that enhance the beauty and dignity of the protagonists. Hector remarks sarcastically upon Paris's good looks and fine hair (Book 3, line 55). Helen's beauty is such that the Trojan elders cannot blame the Greeks and Trojans for fighting over her (Book 3, lines 156–8). Briseis is like golden Aphrodite (Book 19, line 282). When Hector is finally dead, the Greeks marvel at the size and beauty of his body (Book 22, lines 370–1). After they have eaten, Priam expresses his wonder at the stature and beauty of Achilles who is the very image of a god. Achilles in turn admires the appearance of Priam (Book 24, lines 629–33). Heroic excellence is manifested in perfection of physical form. Moral deformity is expressed in physical ugliness as in the case of Thersites who is crook-backed, bald and lame (Book 2, lines 216–19). The value set upon beauty is apparent in the fate of the godlike Ganymede, a mortal who grew to be the most beautiful youth in the world and because of his good looks was stolen by the gods to be cupbearer to Zeus (Book 20, lines 232–5). The gods themselves protect the bodies of their favourites, Sarpedon, Patroclus and Hector, from decay. Their own beauty is taken for granted, and constantly implied by the use of recurring adjectives, for example, golden Aphrodite and Thetis of the silver feet. The most famous Greek sculptor of the fifth century BC is said to have been inspired by the majestic description of the dark eyebrows and ambrosial locks of Zeus at Book 1, lines 528–9, when he made his famous statue of Zeus at Olympia. The description of the messenger of the gods, Hermes, at Book 24, lines 339–48, with his golden sandals and wand, 'looking like a princely youth at the most graceful time when the beard first begins to grow', fits exactly his representation in the statues of later time. The Greek feeling for beauty is fully developed in Homer and can be felt and seen in the style of his visual representations.

The Greeks themselves regarded Homer as the great representative of the grand style in poetry. In a rhetorical treatise on Sublimity (see Critical History), the writer traditionally thought to be called Longinus identifies many passages that he calls **sublime** or grand. Since he is often describing grand conceptions rather than focusing upon linguistic minutiae, what he says can be appreciated by the Greekless reader.

A sublime moment for Longinus is the prayer of Aias in the midst of the struggle to recover the body of Patroclus during which Zeus has enveloped the fight in a dark mist (Book 17, lines 645–7). Longinus comments:

> He does not beg his life, for this plea would be too base for the hero: but since in the crippling darkness he can turn his valour to no noble purpose, he is annoyed that this prevents him from getting on with the fight, and prays for the immediate return of daylight, resolved at least to find a death worthy of his courage, even though Zeus should be fighting against him (Chapter 9, line 10).

Longinus praises, too, representations of divine power, quoting, for example, the moment when Here's horses leap majestically from Olympus to Troy (Book 5, lines 770–2). Such divine actions take us beyond the humdrum everyday world.

Yet perhaps the most obvious stylistic feature of the *Iliad* which can be felt through any version is its energetic fire and its intense animation. When Hector fires the ships, 'He raged like the War-god spear in hand, or like a fire on the mountains' (Book 15, lines 605–6); throughout this episode, he is repeatedly associated in the **similes** and surrounding imagery with the fire that he himself brings to the ships. When Achilles dons his divine armour (Book 19, lines 364ff.), 'his eyes blazed like a fire'; a series of similes follows, magnifying the effect by highlighting the intense glitter of his scintillating arms in an ascending sequence. He is likened first to the moonlight, then to the flames of a beacon, then to a comet, and lastly to the sun itself. When he dashes out for the final encounter (Book 22, lines 22ff.), he runs with the speed of a winning horse and his bronze armour again blazes like a comet portending disease and death.

Similes are a vital element of the ennobling and aggrandising heroic style. The clash of armies is likened to the clash of the elements. Hector and Achilles particularly are likened to fire and in their appearance to the sun and stars. Heroes generally are likened to lions, eagles, falcons, bulls and wild boars. In these similes, nature, whether as elemental force or as animal nature, is not humanised or sentimentalised by use of the **pathetic fallacy**; the opposite is the case. Human beings are associated with the force, majesty and indifference of elemental powers and with the raw power of animal nature in unmitigated and not always admirable aspects. This has the effect of making the actions of the protagonists, however dark they may be, seem like expressions of the life force itself.

However, the narrative does not always feature the obviously beautiful and grand or the awe-inspiring and the terrible. Quite apart from the repulsive detail of the physical horrors of warfare (flies defiling corpses, for example), there are many small circumstances in his poetry, the cry of an infant, descriptions of eating and drinking, the pictures of ordinary life in the similes, boys beating a stubborn ass, flies buzzing about the milk pails in a cowshed or a woman weighing wool. (Here the effect of the similes is to diversify the narrative and link it with a wider world beyond the immediate action.) Homer ranges widely; his grand style is not exclusive.

In his lectures *On Translating Homer* (1861), Matthew Arnold commenting upon the difficulties that Homer presents to translators, offered his famous identification of four characteristic features of Homer's style:

> the translator of Homer should above all be penetrated by a sense of four qualities of his author: – that he is eminently rapid; that he is eminently plain and direct, both in the evolution of his thought and the expression of it, that is, both in his syntax and in his words; that he is eminently plain and direct in the substance of his thought, that is, in his matter and ideas … And yet, in spite of this perfect plainness and directness of his ideas, he is eminently *noble*; he works as entirely in

> the grand style, he is as grandiose, as Phidias [the most famous ancient sculptor of the fourth century BC] or Dante [the great medieval Italian poet (1265–1321) and author of the *Divine Comedy*] or Michael Angelo [the great Renaissance painter and sculptor (1475–1564)]. This is what makes his translators despair. 'To give relief' says Cowper [William Cowper (1731–1800) who translated Homer in the late eighteenth century] 'to prosaic subjects' (such as dressing, eating, drinking, harnessing, travelling, going to bed), that is to treat such subjects nobly, in the grand style, 'without seeming unseasonably tumid, is extremely difficult'. It *is* difficult, but Homer has done it. Homer is precisely the incomparable poet he is, because he has done it. His translation must not be tumid, must not be artificial, must not be literary; true; but then also he must not be commonplace, must not be ignoble.

The traditional **epithets** and formulae like 'bulwark of the Achaeans' pitch the language beyond that of plain and direct prose and there are grand pictures often involving a divine action. Otherwise the poetic effect is largely a consequence of rhythm. In his actual diction and expression Homer, as Arnold says, is plain and direct. He does not use roundabout language (evasive **periphrastical** expressions) to describe everyday things. Wounds, for example, are described with pinpoint accuracy. And not all the descriptions of food and its preparation are formulaic or perfunctory. Nestor provides Patroclus with a wine which has been laced with onion, honey, barley and goat's milk cheese (Book 11, lines 629–41). In all such passages there is realistic detail: Homer dwells on concrete particulars which are clearly and simply represented.

PART FOUR

EXTENDED COMMENTARIES

TEXT 1 (BOOK 6, LINES 440–502)

'All that, my dear,' said the great Hector of the glittering helmet, 'is surely my concern. But if I hid myself like a coward and refused to fight, I could never face the Trojans and the Trojan ladies in their trailing gowns. Besides, it would go against the grain, for I have trained myself always, like a good soldier, to take my place in the front line and win glory for my father and myself. Deep in my heart I know the day is coming when holy Ilium will be destroyed, with Priam and the people of Priam of the good ashen spear. Yet I am not so much distressed by the thought of what the Trojans will suffer, or Hecabe herself, or King Priam, or all my gallant brothers whom the enemy will fling down in the dust, as by the thought of you, dragged off in tears by some Achaean man-at-arms to slavery. I see you there in Argos, toiling for some other woman at the loom, or carrying water from an alien well, a helpless drudge with no will of your own. "There goes the wife of Hector," they will say when they see your tears. "He was the champion of the horse-taming Trojans when Ilium was besieged." And every time they say it, you will feel another pang at the loss of the one man who might have kept you free. Ah, may the earth lie deep on my dead body before I hear the screams you utter as they drag you off!'

As he finished, glorious Hector held out his arms to take his boy. But the child shrank back with a cry to the bosom of his girdled nurse, alarmed by his father's appearance. He was frightened by the bronze of the helmet and the horsehair plume that he saw nodding grimly down at him. His father and his lady mother had to laugh. But noble Hector quickly took his helmet off and put the dazzling thing on the ground. Then he kissed his son, dandled him in his arms, and prayed to Zeus and the other gods: 'Zeus, and you other gods, grant that this boy of mine may be, like me, pre-eminent in Troy; as strong and brave as I; a mighty king of Ilium. May people say, when he comes back from battle, "Here is a better man than his father." Let him bring home the bloodstained armour of the enemy he has killed, and make his mother happy.'

Hector handed the boy to his wife, who took him to her fragrant breast. She was smiling through her tears, and when her husband saw this he was moved. He

> stroked her with his hand and said: 'My dear, I beg you not to be too much distressed. No one is going to send me down to Hades before my proper time. But Fate is a thing that no man born of woman, coward or hero, can escape. Go home now, and attend to your own work, the loom and spindle, and see that the maidservants get on with theirs. War is men's business; and this war is the business of every man in Ilium, myself above all.'
>
> As he spoke, glorious Hector picked up his helmet with its horsehair plume, and his wife set out for home, shedding great tears and with many a backward look. She soon got home, and there in the palace of Hector killer of men she found a number of her women-servants and stirred them all to lamentation. So they mourned for Hector in his own house, though he was still alive, thinking that he would never survive the violence and fury of the Achaeans and come home from the battlefield.

Andromache, fearful for her husband Hector's survival and for her own fate and that of their infant son, has tried to persuade him not to go out to battle. In Hector's reply, he voices his concern for her but expresses the soldier's fear of being branded a coward should he not go out to fight. But it is not simply the fear of public shame that impels him, for he says that it would go against the grain if he were not to fight to seek glory for his father and for himself. His motivation is complex. It is not just duty but also partly desire that impels him. As Homer expresses it, it is his own *thumos* or spirit that orders him to go. Despite the danger and horror of battle, the Homeric heroes, both Greek and Trojan, experience *charma*, joy in the fight. Nevertheless, it is characteristic of Hector that his motivation is expressed moderately; he hopes to win glory for his father Priam as well as for himself. And in this scene he is sympathetic to the feelings of his wife whom he does not rebuke or chastise.

His deep foreboding that Troy will fall and his overriding regret that he will not be able to protect his wife from a future life of drudgery as a slave afford a pitiless and affecting picture of the evil consequences of war to those who are defeated. Present heroism in the poem is always viewed from the perspective of past wrongs and future suffering. Andromache's future humiliation and distress are strongly imagined.

The fright of the child that causes the parents to laugh amidst their sorrows is a small naturalistic detail which creates a familial scene of tender intimacy; it causes Hector to remove his helmet with its nodding plume (a **symbol** of his warrior status that gives rise to one of his **epithets**) so that momentarily he is not the heroic warrior prince but simply a father and husband. Children are a rarity in **epic** poems but Homer's epic conception and style can accommodate the intrusion of quite common details of human experience, including the potentially embarrassing cry of an infant. Nothing could illustrate better the inclusiveness of Homer's grand style.

The prayer to the gods that the son may grow up to excel his father in military prowess is generous on Hector's part, expressing again something moderate and magnanimous in his own character and motivation. Given his foreboding and the reader's knowledge that Troy will fall it is also full of **irony** and **pathos**, for we know that it will not be granted. Later literature records that his son was thrown from the battlements of Troy by Odysseus. Whether this version of events was known to Homer's audience we cannot tell for certain, but after Hector has been killed, the grieving Andromache, addressing her son, imagines his possible fate when 'some Achaean will seize you by the arm and hurl you from the walls to a cruel death' (Book 24, lines 734–5). It is to be presumed then that this prayer was composed by Homer deliberately for pathetic effect.

Hector's attempt to comfort Andromache and to soothe her fears shows a sensitivity not always evinced by military heroes, who have a tendency to expect unquestioning emotional support and a stiff upper lip from wives and those around them. Though he dismisses her and bids her attend to her woman's work, his tone is not harsh or brusque. The assertion of his final words – that no-one is going to send him down to Hades before his time – is an attempt to offer reassurance to Andromache, while at the same time it is an expression of a strain of fatalism that runs through the poem as a whole and is characteristically Greek.

The lamentation for Hector though he is still alive underscores this fatalism. Hector does, of course, come back from the battlefield, having nearly succeeded in firing the ships, but the placing of this scene of tender parting here rather than later, before the final encounter, has the effect of signalling the end even at the poem's beginning; the lamentation casts a long shadow over Hector's success that is to follow.

TEXT 2 (BOOK 14, LINES 346–401)

As he spoke, the Son of Cronos took his Wife in his arms; and the gracious earth sent up fresh grass beneath them, dewy lotus and crocuses, and a soft and crowded bed of hyacinths, to lift them off the ground. In this they lay, covered by a beautiful golden cloud, from which a rain of glistening dew-drops fell.

While the Father lay peacefully on top of Gargarus with his arms round his Wife, conquered by sleep and love, the gentle god of Sleep flew off to the Achaean ships to tell the Earthshaker the news. He went up to the Girdler of the World and unburdened himself of his secret. 'Poseidon,' he said, 'you may help the Danaans now with all your heart and give them the upper hand, if only for a short time, till Zeus wakes up. I sent him into a deep and gentle sleep after Here had tricked him into lying in her arms.'

Sleep then went off to ply his business with the famous nations of mankind, leaving Poseidon more zealous than ever in his championship of the Danaans. He sprang out beyond the front rank to give them his commands. 'Argives,' he cried, 'are we going once more to leave the victory to Hector son of Priam, to let him take the fleet and reap the glory? He says he will; but his only pretext for such boastful talk is the fact that Achilles sits in dudgeon by his hollow ships. Yet Achilles won't be missed so very much, if the rest of us can only rouse ourselves to stand by one another. Listen, all of you, to my plan and carry it out. We must equip ourselves with the best and biggest shields in the camp, put dazzling helmets on our heads, and go into the fight with the longest spears we can lay our hands on. I myself will take command, and I do not think Prince Hector will stand up to us for long, for all his fury. Let every soldier who has proved his worth in battle, but carries a small buckler, hand it over to a weaker man and equip himself with a larger shield.'

They gladly took Poseidon at his word. Wounded as they were, the kings themselves, Tydeides, Odysseus and Agamemnon son of Atreus, prepared their men for the struggle, visiting the ranks and interchanging their arms, so that the best soldiers were now the best equipped, parting with their inferior weapons to inferior troops. When all had donned their gleaming bronze, they set out, with the Earthshaker Poseidon at their head, carrying his long spear and formidable sword in his great hand. This sword is like a lightning flash. It is sacrilege to touch it in battle, and men shrink from it in terror.

> On the other side illustrious Hector brought the Trojans into battle order. And now the most appalling fight of all was staged by Poseidon of the Sable Locks and glorious Hector, one battling for the Argives, the other leading the Trojans on. As they met, with a deafening clamour, the sea washed up to the Argives' huts and ships. But neither the thunder of breakers on the beach, driven in from the deep by a northerly gale; nor the roar of flames when fire attacks the forest in a mountain ravine; nor the wind's moan in the high foliage of the oaks when it rises to a scream in its wrath, is so loud as the terrible war-cry that the Trojans and Achaeans raised as they fell upon each other.

Worried that the Greeks are getting into in serious danger because Zeus is keeping his promise to Thetis and allowing the Trojans success (we are reminded later in this extract that Diomedes, Odysseus and Agamemnon are wounded), Here has seduced Zeus and with the aid of the god Sleep has laid him to rest so that she and Poseidon can freely give aid to the Greeks.

The message of Sleep to Poseidon does not attempt to disguise what the god describes as Here's trick. In behaving so scandalously, the gods diversify the narrative and provide some relief, often with comic overtones, from the intensity of the fighting. In this extract, the opening lines, describing their bed on Gargarus, the peak on Mount Ida from which Zeus had previously been surveying the fighting, create an image of magical beauty in sharp contrast to what is to come. At the same time the actions of the gods, as they work at cross purposes with one another, are a means of introducing clear changes in the general direction of the action. Poseidon's help halts the Trojans and puts heart into the Greeks so that the divine intervention is a way of initiating turns in the plot.

Poseidon gives a rousing speech of encouragement and offers a clear plan. The Greeks are to concentrate their resources by seeing that the best fighters have the best equipment. This is actually a good idea, a fully rational plan that makes entire sense on the human plane. That is to say, it could have been suggested by the Greek leaders themselves as the best tactic under the circumstances. In fact the plan is immediately put into action by the Greek leaders as they visit the ranks and organise an exchange of arms. Divine intervention, therefore, does not necessarily undermine the integrity and probability of the human action. The effect of it is simply to reinforce it and to make it more vivid.

This reinforcement of the narrative and its emphatic visual enhancement are apparent in the description of the resulting army as it sets out. The picture of Poseidon at the army's head is obviously one of immense power, concentrated in the image of his sword which is like a 'lightning flash'. It is a special sword which it is sacrilege to touch and one that inspires mortal terror. Poseidon, master of the seas, is usually associated with the trident but here he appropriately carries a sword which represents the newly organised fighting power of the land army. That fighting power is raised in the audience's imagination through its representation in the divine image of special power and terror. However petty the gods and goddesses may often be in their motivation and behaviour, in their appearance and action in the war they always have an enhancing effect. Without the presence of Poseidon here, the narrative of the Greek leaders putting their plan into action and marching out to meet the foe would be merely routine.

The magnifying enhancement of the divine presence makes credible what follows when the deafening clamour of the armies as they meet is said to be greater than thunder or a roaring forest fire or a northern storm-wind shrieking through the woods. Such **similes**, likening the noise of the armies to the loudest elemental forces, might in some narratives seem overblown and exaggerated, but here they follow on quite easily and naturally from the image of power and terror encapsulated in the image of the god with his sword. The inclusion of the divine, therefore, is one of the essential means by which Homer creates and sustains the grandeur of the **epic**.

TEXT 3 (BOOK 22, LINES 306–66)

Hanging down at his side, Hector had a sharp, long and weighty sword. He drew this now, braced himself, and swooped like a high-flying eagle that drops to earth through the black clouds to pounce on a tender lamb or a crouching hare. Thus Hector charged, brandishing his sharp sword. Achilles sprang to meet him, inflamed with savage passion. He kept his front covered with his decorated shield; his glittering helmet with its four plates swayed as he moved his head and made the splendid golden plumes that Hephaestus had lavished on the crest dance round the top; and bright as the loveliest jewel in the sky, the Evening Star when he comes out at nightfall with the rest, the sharp point scintillated on the spear he balanced in his right hand, intent on killing Hector, and searching him for the likeliest place to reach his flesh.

Achilles saw that Hector's body was completely covered by the fine bronze armour he had taken from the great Patroclus when he killed him, except for an opening at the gullet where the collar bones lead over from the shoulders to the neck, the easiest place to kill a man. As Hector charged him, Prince Achilles drove at this spot with his lance; and the point went right through the tender flesh of Hector's neck, though the heavy bronze head did not cut his windpipe, and left him able to address his conqueror. Hector came down in the dust and the great Achilles triumphed over him. 'Hector,' he said, 'no doubt you fancied as you stripped Patroclus that you would be safe. You never thought of me: I was too far away. You were a fool. Down by the hollow ships there was a man far better than Patroclus in reserve, the man who has brought you low. So now the dogs and birds of prey are going to maul and mangle you, while we Achaeans hold Patroclus' funeral.'

'I beseech you,' said Hector of the glittering helmet in a failing voice, 'by your knees, by your own life and by your parents, not to throw my body to the dogs at the Achaean ships, but to take a ransom for me. My father and my lady mother will pay you bronze and gold in plenty. Give up my body to be taken home, so that the Trojans and their wives may honour me in death with the ritual of fire.'

The swift Achilles scowled at him. 'You cur,' he said, 'don't talk to me of knees or name my parents in your prayers. I only wish that I could summon up the appetite to carve and eat you raw myself, for what you have done to me. But this at least is certain, that nobody is going to keep the dogs from you, not even if the Trojans bring here and weigh out a ransom ten or twenty times your worth, and promise more besides; not if Dardanian Priam tells them to pay your weight in gold – not even so shall your lady mother lay you on a bier to mourn the son she bore, but the dogs and birds of prey shall eat you up.'

Hector of the flashing helmet spoke to him once more at the point of death. 'How well I know you and can read your mind!' he said. 'Your heart is hard as iron – I have been wasting my breath. Nevertheless, pause before you act, in case the angry gods remember how you treated me, when your turn comes and you are brought down at the Scaean Gate in all your glory by Paris and Apollo.'

> Death cut Hector short and his disembodied soul took wing for the House of Hades, bewailing its lot and the youth and manhood that it left. But Prince Achilles spoke to him again though he was gone. 'Die!' he said. 'As for my own death, let it come when Zeus and the other deathless gods decide.'

In the climactic action of the poem, the final encounter of Achilles and Hector, the Trojan has just realised that the gods are not on his side and that he is about to die. The final movement in their long contest is full of vivid action. The dynamic verbs speak for themselves: 'swooped', 'pounce', 'charged', 'brandishing', 'sprang'. The **simile** likening Hector to the eagle, king of birds, itself is swift. This is not a moment for an extended comparison: all is concentrated on the action at hand. Hector thrusts and Achilles protects himself with his shield. The movement continues in the image of the splendid golden plumes dancing round the crest of his helmet. Achilles is enhanced by mention of the god who had made his arms, the splendour of which is further enhanced by the simile in which his spear scintillates like the evening star. The description of the glittering appearance keeps the narrative at a pitch of elevation.

The actual killing is realistic in the sense that Achilles sees the point of vulnerability and aims accordingly; it is not achieved through an improbable piercing of armour or even as a result of his divinely made weaponry. As Hector is wearing Achilles's former armour which he had despoiled from the body of Patroclus, the warriors both have divinely made armour and are in this respect evenly matched. The mortal blow is not in itself the climax of the encounter, indeed it could be said that the poet is more focused upon the emotions of Achilles here than upon his physical actions, since the killing is narrated quickly and does not show the kind of ingenious physical resource that the Greek hero had earlier shown in his contest with the river god Scamander. The death blow which leaves Hector still able to speak is the prelude to the final exchange of words between the two heroes which is the poet's chief interest.

Achilles exults over the defeated foe in the usual way allowed by the heroic code but there is little real triumph in his words. His bitter mockery of Hector is preoccupied at the beginning and end with his feelings for Patroclus. He mocks what he imagines was Hector's blind moment of triumph when he was oblivious of Achilles, rebuking Hector for forgetting that there was a better man left than Patroclus (a stronger warrior, that is) and takes pleasure in drawing a distinction between Hector's exposure to the dogs and birds and the funeral that the Greeks will be holding for Patroclus.

In reply, Hector repeats his plea that Achilles allow decent burial to his body. His talk of ransom raises the issue that will now dominate the remainder of the poem. In rejecting this plea for what is according to the highest standards of the heroic code every person's due right, Achilles shows no slackening at all of his intense anger. The killing brings no immediate satisfaction; revenge is not sweet. The extremity of his wish that he could summon up the appetite to eat Hector's raw flesh himself, the absolute determination to reject the possibility of any ransom however large, and his conscious desire to deny Hector's mother the chance to lay her son on a bier – all this is the expression of someone who is still beside himself and deaf to all human pleas.

Just as Patroclus had prophesied the death of Hector in his dying speech, so the final words of Hector foretell the death of Achilles at the hands of Paris (who shot him in the heel with an arrow). Replying, Achilles, who already knows that his life will be short, accepts his own death in fatalistic resignation to the will of Zeus.

The death of Hector is not therefore an occasion of glory or triumph for Achilles, nor does it bring the sweet satisfaction of revenge. The recent death of Patroclus which continues to haunt his consciousness and the imminence of his own death preclude any note of triumph or joy in victory.

Part five

Background

The Homeric Question

Nothing is known for certain about the authorship of the *Iliad* or about its date and place of composition. Indeed all the circumstances surrounding the composition and early transmission of the Homeric poems are matters of surmise and controversy that together have come to be known as the 'Homeric Question'. It is unlikely that a satisfactory solution to the problem, that has greatly perplexed scholars and critics alike for nearly two centuries, will ever now be found. The literature upon the subject is very considerable and all that can be done here is to indicate some of the main difficulties and to record the latest consensus of scholarly opinion. That consensus may be more apparent than real and at best can only offer a likely theory.

The *Iliad* and the *Odyssey* are the oldest surviving texts in Greek literature. There are no internal references to their author or to their origin and there are no other contemporary documents to throw light upon them. They exist in what is virtually an historical vacuum. Nor is there any reliable tradition about their origin in the earliest Greek literature following them. The Greeks all agree on the name 'Homer' and there is a persistent tradition that, like the bard Demodocus in the *Odyssey*, he was blind, but different views are recorded concerning his date and birthplace. Seven cities claimed to be the birthplace of Homer, the most favoured in antiquity being Chios and Smyrna, both in the region of Ionia in the eastern Aegean. The Greeks believed in the historical reality of the Trojan War, but the reliability of the Homeric version was questioned. According to some accounts Homer was a contemporary witness of events; according to others his poem was composed some time after the fall of Troy, an event which in any case was for the earliest Greek historians shrouded in the mists of prehistory.

Any consideration of the Homeric Question must begin with the picture of the Homeric bard in the *Odyssey*. There are two bards in the poem, Phemius, resident in the palace of Odysseus in Ithaca, and the blind Demodocus who resides in the palace of King Alcinous in Phaeacia, which is visited by Odysseus in the course of his wanderings from Troy. Both bards have an honoured place and sing to the accompaniment of the lyre. Phemius sings of the woes inflicted on the Greeks returning from Troy (Book 1, lines 326–7). Demodocus sings three short songs, the first of which is about a quarrel between the leading Greeks at the beginning of the Trojan story (Book 8, lines 73–82). The second is a comic tale about the gods (lines 266–366). The third is at the request of Odysseus, who commends Demodocus for his truthfulness in faithfully recording the memory of the sufferings of the Greeks at Troy and asks him to sing of the Wooden Horse, the stratagem by which the Greeks took Troy. Demodocus, stirred by the god of song, begins from the point at which the Greeks sailed away (line 500). He tells how the Trojans took the huge horse into the city thinking that the Greeks had departed, and how the Greeks hidden inside it came out at night and sacked the city (lines 487–520). The implication is that Demodocus knows many songs about gods and heroes and that in particular he knows the whole Trojan story which he can take up at any point. Moreover, it is implied that the bard transmits faithfully the memory of the great events of the past. Later in the poem Phemius boasts to Odysseus that he is self-taught and knows many different songs. The poet of the *Iliad* and *Odyssey* must be a literary descendant of the Homeric bard as he appears in the *Odyssey*. But Demodocus and Phemius work on a small scale, reciting single tales. There is no hint in either the *Iliad* or the *Odyssey* of an occasion which could have prompted the composition of poems of such great length and scope.

How could the poems have been transmitted? Early literary sources report the existence of a guild called the Homeridae who, claiming to be the descendants of Homer, flourished in Chios and were devoted to the recitation of his poems. In addition there were other professional reciters of Homer's poetry called ***rhapsodes***. Their existence is well attested, and they recited Homer's poetry from memory at public festivals and games where they competed with one another for prizes. Again it is difficult to imagine an occasion on which the poems might have been recited in their entirety.

It was the lack of any known occasion for the composition of poems of this length, together with the difficulty of explaining how poems of this length and artistic unity could have been composed without the aid of writing, that led the German Homeric scholar Friedrich Wolf (1759–1824) to raise the Homeric Question. It is not that Wolf denied the existence of 'Homer'. He believed that Homer had existed and had initiated the poems in their early form. But he declared in his *Prolegomena ad Homerum* of 1795 that the Homeric poems as we know them did not have a single author but had progressively evolved as successive *rhapsodes* added and developed what had come down to them. Some ancient scholars known as the *chorizontes* or separators had believed that the *Iliad* and the *Odyssey* were by different authors, and some ancient commentators had suspected that particular lines and even some episodes had been interpolated, but it was not until Wolf that unity of authorship of the individual poems was fundamentally questioned.

Wolf's theory arose primarily from a consideration of the external factors mentioned above. After him the poems themselves were rigorously analysed. Internal discrepancies and inconsistencies were seen to be evidence of multiple authorship. During this time even those who disagreed with Wolf's conclusions accepted that the *Iliad* and *Odyssey* had come into being gradually over a period of time, since it is apparent that like a rock face they contain various layers of material, some of which must be given a comparatively late date while some belong to earlier time.

ARCHAEOLOGY & THE HOMERIC POEMS

The ancient Greeks had believed in the substantial reality of Homer's world, but students of Homer from the eighteenth century onwards tended to believe that the material world of Homer and the events he described were poetic fictions, until in the later part of the nineteenth century archaeologists began to reconstruct the early history of civilisation in the Mediterranean from the physical evidence provided by excavations. The most famous name in Homeric archaeology is that of the German scholar Heinrich Schliemann (1822–90) who excavated what he believed to be the site of Troy at Hissarlik in northern Turkey in the early 1870s. His conviction that he had found Homer's Troy has not always been shared by subsequent archaeologists. He later excavated Mycenae (1876) and Tiryns (1884) on the Greek mainland. Other places mentioned in

Homer, notably Pylos, were investigated by other archaeologists. Shortly after 1900 Sir Arthur Evans (1851–1941) excavated Cnossus in Crete, and these early archaeological endeavours provided the foundations for new knowledge about ancient Greece in the period preceding the earliest literary records. This new knowledge has tended to suggest that the culture and events of the Homeric poems have some basis in historical truth.

The island of Crete is the earliest centre of civilisation in the Mediterranean. The remains at Cnossus show that the Bronze Age civilisation called Minoan (from Minos, the mythical lawgiver of Crete) was highly developed and lasted from roughly 3000 to 1000BC. In mainland Greece, a Bronze Age civilisation, centred upon royal palaces such as those excavated at Mycenae, Tiryns and Pylos, developed somewhat later and lasted from 1580 to 1120BC. This civilisation is called Mycenaean, after what seems to have been its most powerful centre, Mycenae. In Homer, Agamemnon, leader of the Greek expedition to Troy and the most powerful of the Greek princes, comes from Mycenae which Homer calls 'rich in gold', 'broad-streeted' and 'well built'. In the Catalogue of Ships in Book 2 of the *Iliad* the largest numbers come from Mycenae and Pylos.

A script known as Linear B, on clay tablets found at Pylos, Mycenae and Cnossus, establishes strong links between Minoan and Mycenaean civilisations, and the decipherment of the script in the 1950s established that their common language was an archaic form of Greek. The extant tablets record accounts and inventories that have to do with the routine administration of the royal palaces. How widely the script was known and used cannot be ascertained. There is no evidence that it was used to record literature. The script is, comparatively speaking, a cumbersome one and could hardly have been used for a literary work of the length of the *Iliad*, even supposing that suitable materials such as leather or parchment were available. Nevertheless the existence of the script is an indication of the developed material culture of Mycenaean Greece.

After the destruction of Cnossus in 1400BC, Mycenaean civilisation was at its most powerful and advanced. The most substantial remains at Mycenae, the so-called Treasury of Atreus and the Tomb of Clytemnestra (Atreus was the father of Agamemnon and Clytemnestra was his wife) were built after 1300BC and the Lion Gate of Mycenae (so called from the relief over its lintel) dates from 1250BC. The fortification walls were mighty indeed. They were between twelve and forty-five feet thick and it has been estimated that they were as high as forty feet. The treasures found by Schliemann in the royal graves at Mycenae, which include the famous gold face masks, bear witness to the opulent beauty of Mycenaean art work which was highly sophisticated in its craftsmanship and design. The techniques of engraving, enchasing and embossing were well developed and so was the art of inlaying bronze with precious metals. Ivory and amber imported from the east and the north are commonly found and indicate the extent of Mycenaean commercial relations. Mycenaean pottery of this period is found widely throughout the Mediterranean, a further indication that the Mycenaeans were great sailors and traders.

Excavations at Hissarlik, the site of Troy, have revealed nine settlements, the sixth settlement having substantial fortifications and monumental walls. The seventh of these settlements was destroyed in a great fire in the mid-thirteenth century BC, so that archaeological evidence seems to support the possibility of an historical Trojan War of which the Homeric account records the poetic memory. Soon after this possible date for the fall of Troy, Mycenaean power began to decline until, in about 1120BC, Mycenae and Tiryns and with them the Mycenaean culture of the Bronze Age were destroyed by the Dorians invading from the north. The Dorians were themselves Greek-speaking and possibly lived on the fringe of the Mycenaean empire. They initiated what is usually known as the Dark Ages, lasting from 1100 to 800BC. The Bronze Age gave way to the new Age of Iron. Refugees from the dispersal in mainland Greece created by the Dorian invasion now began to colonise the eastern seaboard of the Aegean Sea known as Ionia in Asia Minor. The Homeric poems are generally considered to have been composed in Ionia (largely on linguistic grounds); they may therefore preserve the memory of the Mycenaean mother culture transmitted by those who had colonised Asia Minor.

There are certainly relics of Mycenaean culture in the *Iliad*. It is generally agreed that the Catalogue of Ships in Book 2 is of early origin, and some scholars believe that it describes Greece as it was known in Mycenaean times. A more specific instance of a Mycenaean survival is the boar's tusk helmet of Odysseus described at Book 10, lines 261–5. It is of a kind that is found in Mycenaean tombs and is not to be found in later excavations. The long body shield of Aias worn without body armour (Book 7, lines 219–32) is Mycenaean and was gradually replaced by the smaller round shield with which a protective breastplate was worn. Homer mentions both kinds of armour. The historical mixture in the Homeric poems is well suggested by the use in them of both bronze and iron. Bronze is the principal metal used for armour and tools, but the heads of Pandarus's arrows are iron (Book 4, line 123). Familiarity with iron is apparent in the use of it as a **metaphor**. When King Priam proposes to visit Achilles, his wife Hecabe exclaims that he must have a heart of iron (Book 24, line 205) to visit the camp of the man who has killed so many of their sons. When Priam actually arrives, Achilles repeats the exclamation (Book 24, line 521). The Homeric poems also record practices and customs that differ from those of Mycenaean times. For example, the Mycenaeans buried their dead, while in Homer the dead are cremated. In Mycenaean warfare one spear was used while Homer's warriors habitually carry two. Experts on warfare note that the tactics employed at Book 13, lines 131–5 imply the use of the phalanx, an organised line of hoplites (infantrymen) that did not come into being until the development of the city state, possibly suggesting a date as late as 800BC. Some have thought that the scenes from ordinary life in the **similes** are those of Homer's own day and that Homer is deliberately drawing parallels between a heroic past and a humble present.

THE LANGUAGE OF HOMER

Historians of the Greek language have identified the same kind of layered structure as that revealed by the archaeologists, in which archaic elements co-exist side by side with later Ionic forms. The language of Homer is a fusion of elements from various dialects, the chief of which are the Ionic, the Aeolic, and the Arcadian. The predominant element is the Ionic, and this is the main reason for believing that the Homeric poems emanate from Ionia, but the Arcadian and Aeolic forms and vocabulary suggest that the Homeric **epic** has its roots in earlier times. The Arcadian and Aeolic dialects developed from dialects of Greek spoken in mainland Greece in the south and north respectively during the Mycenaean period.

The fusion of these dialects with the Ionic has contributed to the view that Ionic bards took over and adapted to new circumstances and a new audience material which they had inherited from the past.

It is not simply the fusion of different dialect forms and vocabulary which suggests that the language of the Homeric poems has a long and complicated history. Study of Homeric composition has revealed a highly sophisticated process at work which can only have been refined over a long period of time. The process involves the development and use of **formulae**, the stock-in-trade of the **oral poet** who composed without the aid of writing. Some recurring Homeric formulae have become world-famous like 'the wine-dark sea', 'rosy-fingered dawn' or 'winged words'. Formulae may be short phrases like the above or may extend to longer passages describing often repeated actions such as the arming for battle, the preparation of a meal or the ritual of sacrifice. Formulae are convenient units that can be readily committed to memory and are therefore an aid to improvisation for the oral poet who is wholly dependent upon memory. In a famous study of Homeric formulae in the 1920s the American Homeric scholar Milman Parry (1902–35) demonstrated both the scope and economy of the system of formulaic composition.

It is necessary to have some rudimentary knowledge of Greek metre and the structure of the Greek language to understand how the formulaic system works. Homer's metre is the **hexameter**, a metre of six units (called feet); it is an arrangement of long and short syllables according to fixed rules. Greek metre is quantitative, that is, words are fitted into the metrical pattern according to length of syllable. (In English metre the pattern is determined by accent, by the stress given to words in pronunciation.) The scansion of the hexameter is as follows:

– u u	– u u	– u u	– u u	– u u	– –
– –	– –	– –	– –		– u

A long syllable followed by two short ones (sounding like tum ti ti) is called a **dactyl** (hence Homer's metre is often known as the dactylic hexameter) and two long syllables together are called a **spondee** (tum tum). The first four feet may be either dactyls or spondees (with usually more dactyls than spondees). The fifth must be a dactyl and the final foot is never a dactyl but the second syllable may be short, thus making a

trochee (tum ti). This recurring rhythmical pattern at the end of the line in the fifth and sixth foot (a recurring tum ti ti tum tum or tum ti ti tum ti) creates a regular rise and fall and gives an effect not wholly unlike that of rhyme, though rhyme itself is never used in Homer nor indeed in any classical Greek or Latin poetry.

Greek is an inflected language, so that the forms of nouns and adjectives change according to the particular case in question, whether nominative, vocative, accusative, genitive, or dative. (In an inflected language there are naturally many similar sounds at the ends of words, as adjectives have the same case as the nouns they qualify. This may account for the avoidance of rhyme schemes in classical literature.) Homer uses a number of adjectives to describe the hero of the *Iliad*, Achilles. All these adjectives are generally appropriate to his character and role. But what Parry demonstrated is that in any particular context what governs the choice of a particular adjective is above all a metrical consideration. In the nominative case, when he is the subject of a sentence, Achilles is illustrious or swift-footed. He is only ever swift-footed in the nominative case. In the vocative, when anyone is addressing him, he is godlike. In the accusative when he is the object of a sentence he is illustrious. In the genitive case when he is possessing something he is always the son of Peleus. In the dative case when anyone is giving anything to him he is the shepherd of his people or a sacker of cities. The various noun/adjective combinations (sometimes there can be more than one adjective, for he can be both swift and illustrious together in the nominative case) all make different metrical patterns so that they can be slotted into the metre in different places. Each of these combinations is determined by the case of the noun and by the position that the noun has in the verse, but no one of these combinations duplicates another; they are all metrically different. The scope is evident in the large number of combinations which have been developed to meet any syntactical and metrical need. The economy is evident in the fact that each of these combinations is unique, metrically speaking, and therefore allows the poet great flexibility in expression. Metre in any poetry determines what can and what cannot be said. What is remarkable about Parry's analysis of Homeric composition is that it suggests the restrictions inherent in oral composition and the extraordinary technical virtuosity through which they have been overcome.

The formulaic character of the Homeric epic can explain how it is that there are various layers, the earliest of which transmit relics of Mycenaean times. The oldest linguistic elements are probably what have come to be known as the 'traditional **epithets**', such as 'ox-eyed Here', 'cloud-gathering Zeus' or 'Alalkomenaean Athene', some of which perplexed the Greeks themselves. The first systematic study of Homer in the late sixth century seems to have been concerned with the need to explain obsolete and difficult words. The formulaic character also explains why Homer's adjectives occasionally seem inappropriate in their particular context, why, for example, the sky is starry in the middle of the day (Book 8, line 46). Finally, the formulaic character of the epic goes some way to explain the obvious fact of repetition. About one third of the lines in the *Iliad* are repeated wholly or in part in the course of the poem. Equally one third is made up of phrases not found elsewhere. It is clear that the traditional inheritance was constantly being added to and varied to meet contemporary needs and the requirements of different tales. Homer's language therefore had been purposely developed for poetic recitation; it was never a spoken language. Nor did such a development, any more than the myths or the tales themselves, originate with one genius. There is a consensus of scholarly opinion that the language of the *Iliad* and *Odyssey* evolved over many centuries and that its technique of formulaic diction goes back to the Mycenaean age from which it was no doubt transmitted by practising bards like Demodocus and Phemius in the *Odyssey*.

Some problems

But here the consensus stops and the Homeric question remains. The poetic excellence of the Homeric poems presupposes individual talent. Nobody can believe that countless other poems of the quality of the *Iliad* and *Odyssey* have been lost to us. Where does the individual talent stand in relation to the tradition? Most would say that 'Homer' came at the end of it. But was he a fully **oral poet** like Demodocus and Phemius, or did he use the oral method simply because he was composing for recitation? Did he dictate the text to a scribe, or did he write it himself? These are all open questions.

SOME PROBLEMS continued

Comparisons with oral **epics** in other cultures show that in preliterate cultures feats of memory that would be considered to be astonishing in a literate culture are common enough. Bards have recited from memory, or have improvised poems that are longer than the *Iliad*. But such poems are comparatively crude and do not have either the complex structure or the finished artistry of the Homeric poems. The difference in quality between the Homeric poems and oral epics in other cultures is more significant than anything that they have in common.

The problem is not made any easier by the inconclusive results of attempts to provide a date for the poems. The various layers that are apparent in the *Iliad* have been so fused that neither linguists nor archaeologists have been able to unravel the puzzle. Book 10 of the *Iliad* on various, chiefly linguistic, grounds has been thought to be 'late', even by the ancient Greeks themselves. Yet **ironically** it contains what archaeologists recognise as one of the most obvious Mycenaean relics in the boar's tusk helmet worn by Odysseus. Nor have archaeologists been able to identify and provide a date for the most recent physical object in the poem. Most authorities envisage a date somewhere in the eighth century BC for the composition of the poems. Nor is it known for certain when writing was introduced to Greece.

Evidence suggests that knowledge and use of the syllabic Linear B script referred to earlier did not survive the fall of Mycenaean civilisation in the late twelfth century BC. Sometime between the tenth century and the eighth a new alphabetic script from Phoenicia was adopted in Greece. Papyrus (a form of paper originating in Egypt) seems not to have been introduced until later. Leather is known to have been used for writing quite early, though it would have been a costly business to commit a poem the size of the *Iliad* to leather. Any kind of book remained a rarity until the fifth century. Nevertheless the materials were available and it is theoretically possible that the poems were committed to writing at an early stage.

THE HISTORY OF THE WRITTEN TEXT

The earliest written text of Homer for which there is any evidence in Greek sources dates from the late sixth century BC when the Athenian leader of the day is reported to have brought texts of the poems to Athens and to have required the ***rhapsodes*** who recited Homer's poetry at the annual Athenian festival to do so one after another in proper order so that the poems would be recited as a whole. Given the special status of Homer in Greek culture from the earliest times, attested in the formation of special guilds of *rhapsodes* to recite the poems, it is certainly credible that there was a need for a definitive text.

The first textual criticism of Homer was carried out in the third and second centuries BC in the famous library at Alexandria by a succession of scholars, the most notable of whom was Aristarchus (*c.*215–145BC). Many texts of Homer had been collected for the Alexandrian library and divergencies in the number of lines and variations in wording were glaringly apparent. At this time the Homeric text was standardised, and each poem was split up into twenty-four books, each given a letter of the Greek alphabet and a title heading still used to this day. This text standardised at Alexandria is the ancestor of all the texts that have come down to the modern world.

The Alexandrian version was copied like other ancient texts on papyrus rolls until the late second century AD when the codex (a book with pages) was introduced and papyrus was gradually replaced by the more durable parchment. The oldest surviving complete manuscripts are medieval, but fragments of the poems on papyrus survive from Graeco-Roman times. Some manuscripts preserve the opinions of the ancient commentators and the notes of Alexandrian textual critics in the form of **scholia**, comments written in the margins above and beside the text. Similar material is also incorporated in compilations made by Byzantine scholars from collections of material now lost. The most notable of these compilations is the vast commentary on the poems made sometime in the twelfth century by Eustathius, Archbishop of Thessalonika. These Byzantine commentaries, the scholia and ancient papyri have all been used by modern textual critics to arrive at the best possible text of the Homeric poems.

Part six

Critical history & further reading

Greek responses

Plato, Aristotle & Longinus

From the beginning, Homer occupied a central position in the culture of the Greeks. It has been said in fact that Homer was the Bible of the Greeks. The earliest criticism of Homer came as the mythical view of the world embodied in the Homeric poems was challenged by philosophers, who particularly found fault in the Homeric depiction of the gods. Defenders of Homer resorted to **allegory** to prove that under the veil of fiction Homer was really a good philosopher. In its fable as a whole, the *Iliad*, unlike the *Odyssey*, resisted allegorical interpretation, but the approach might be tried with the parts. In Book 1, for example, Apollo sends a plague, which causes the Greeks to meet in an assembly, in which the leaders quarrel to a point where the goddess Athene has to intervene to prevent Achilles from killing Agamemnon. Allegorically, since Apollo is the sun god, the plague is caused by a heatwave; since Athene is the goddess of wisdom her intervention may be regarded as a way of representing the triumph of reason over passion. Allegorical interpretation had long been established by the time of Plato, who distrusted it on the grounds that it is the surface meaning that impresses, and in the most celebrated philosophical attack upon the Homeric poems he expresses the belief in his *Republic* that Homer had told lies about the gods and had misrepresented the heroic world, showing the heroes in a bad light (377e, 383a 386a ff.). Believing that the Homeric poems were a bad influence that encouraged emotional excess, he banished Homer from his ideal state (*Republic* 606e).

In his *Poetics* (*c*.340BC), Aristotle is mostly concerned about **tragedy** but he has scattered remarks on Homer that have become famous (see Chapters 8, 17, 23 and 24). Given the shaping influence of Homer on Greek art and culture, it is hardly surprising that, in his comments on **unity** in a work of art, his touchstone is Homer. He points out that a work of art does not have a unity simply because it deals with one character because many different things happen to a character that do not necessarily make up a unity. Homer whether through instinct or knowledge of his art knew this when he made the poem cohere in a single action (Chapters 8 and 23).

> Homer may seem divinely inspired, in that even with the Trojan war, which has a beginning and an end, he did not attempt to dramatise it as a whole, since it would have either been too long to be taken in all at once or, if he had moderated the length, he would have complicated it by the variety of incident. As it is, he takes one part of the story only and uses many episodes from other parts, such as the Catalogue of Ships and other episodes of that kind (Chapter 23).

He also remarks that the *Iliad* is a simple story turning upon calamity (the Greek word is *pathetikon*), whereas the *Odyssey* is complex, being full of discoveries (***anagnorisis***) and turns on character (*ethike*) (Chapter 24).

In later writers the idea developed from this distinction that in the *Iliad* Homer was the father of tragedy while in the *Odyssey* with its depiction of justice and a happy ending he was the father of comedy.

In the treatise *On the Sublime* attributed to a rhetorician named Longinus (of uncertain date), Homer is a frequent touchstone exemplifying the **sublime** or the grand in style. Most of his examples are from the *Iliad* which he regarded as the more sublime. In fact his comparison of the two poems, in which he seems to use Aristotle's distinctions, has become famous. He judged the *Odyssey* with its penchant for narrative and romance inferior to the *Iliad* with its vigorous action and 'strong tide of motions and passions'. He praises its dramatic action and sustained energy, 'the consistent sublimity that never sinks into flatness', and 'the versatile rapidity and actuality, brimful of images drawn from real life' (Chapter 9, 13). Many of his examples feature descriptions and actions of the gods. He admires Homer's imaginative genius in his Battle of the Gods, yet, even as a critic sympathetic to Homer, finds the Homeric depiction of the gods sometimes difficult to bear:

> Awe-inspiring as these passages are, from another aspect, if they are not taken as allegory, they are altogether ungodly, and do not preserve our sense of what is fitting. In his accounts of the wounds suffered by the gods, their quarrels, their vengeful actions, their tears, their imprisonment, and all their manifold passions,

> Homer seems to me to have done everything in his power to make gods of the men fighting at Troy, and men of the gods (Chapter 9, 7).

HOMERIC QUESTIONS & PROBLEMS

Most of the early criticism of Homer related to his thematic content, particularly his depiction of the gods, but from earliest times adverse judgements were also made about aspects of his art. In antiquity books were produced of Homeric problems, in which problems were raised and solutions discussed. Some of these questions were niggling and silly, reflecting the philistinism of those who made them. Such hypercriticism is associated with the name of Zoilus, a critic of Homer living in the fourth century BC. Others raised genuine problems which have since become part of the larger Homeric Question. What were earlier seen as artistic weaknesses or oddities have lately come to be regarded as points of evidence against unity of authorship in the arguments of analytical critics. A representative selection of the commonest points that have been debated about the *Iliad*, most but not all having a possible bearing upon the Homeric Question, and some of them of the niggling kind, is listed below in an order suggested by the arrangement of the poem itself.

- Apollo and Athene take part in the action of Book 1. Thetis later tells Achilles that all the gods are away feasting in Ethiopia for twelve days. What is to be made of this inconsistency?
- What is the point of Agamemnon's test of the army (Book 2, line 73)? Is it adequately motivated?
- Why should Priam need to be told about the Greek leaders in the tenth year of the siege of Troy (Book 3, lines 161–242)?
- In the council on Olympus (Book 4, lines 1–72), why is no reference made to Zeus's promise to Thetis?
- Pylaemenes killed at Book 5, line 576 is alive at Book 13, line 658. What conclusion can be drawn from this inconsistency?
- 'If you are a god, I am not the sort to fight against the immortals', says Diomedes (Book 6, lines 128–9) to the unknown Glaucus, having just wounded Aphrodite and Ares (in Book 5). What is to be made of this apparent inconsistency?

- In the exchange between Hector and Paris (Book 6, lines 313–41) no mention is made of the latter's recent duel with Menelaus (Book 3). Is this not puzzling?
- Why should the Greeks agree to a second duel (Book 7, lines 91–102) after the Trojans have broken their oaths in the first?
- Why should it suddenly occur to the Greeks in the tenth year of the siege to build a defensive wall to protect their ships at a time when they are winning?
- Is the inexorability of Achilles in Book 9 consistent with his later attitudes (in Books 11 and 16)?
- Why is Phoenix, Achilles's old retainer, with Agamemnon and not with Achilles (Book 9, line 168)?
- Are the actions of Diomedes and Odysseus in Book 10 consistent with the standards of behaviour that are shown in the rest of the poem as the accepted norm in the heroic world?
- Does Nestor's long account of his youthful prowess (Book 11, lines 656–762) serve any useful purpose in its context?
- Poseidon has been helping the Greeks quite successfully in Book 13. Is the deception of Zeus in Book 14 (a) necessary, or (b) should it have come earlier?
- How successfully does Homer keep the reader's interest during the fighting in the middle section of the poem (Books 12–15)?
- 'Attend while I tell you what to do so that all the Greeks may honour me and restore the lovely girl and give splendid gifts' (Book 16, lines 83–6). How do these words of Achilles to Patroclus stand in relation to the embassy to Achilles in Book 9?
- Why does Homer delay (until Book 18) the bringing of the news of Patroclus's death to Achilles?
- After the magnificent return of Achilles to the fighting, is not the encounter with Aeneas (Book 20, lines 79–352) with its long conversation and lack of vigorous action an anticlimax?
- Is the battle of the gods (Book 20, lines 385–513) consistent with the dignity of epic?
- Would the poem be better without the last two books, thus ending with the climactic action of the death of Hector?

FURTHER READING

Howard Clarke, *Homer's Readers*, University of Delaware Press, 1981

Contains a substantial chapter on 'Homer Allegorised'

A.H. Gilbert, ed., *Literary Criticism: Plato to Dryden*, Wayne State University Press, 1962

Includes the relevant extracts from Plato's *Republic* together with other ancient and Renaissance criticism. Usefully indexed

T.S. Dorsch, translator, *Classical Literary Criticism*, Penguin Books. 1965

Contains Aristotle's *Poetics* and Longinus's *On the Sublime*

TRANSLATIONS & REWORKINGS

Translation may be regarded as a form of interpretation that itself may involve a critical assessment of the original, and Homer has been much translated. The two most famous English versions are those of George Chapman (*c*.1559–1634) whose complete version of the *Iliad* was published in 1611 and Alexander Pope (1688–1744) published in 1715–20. Chapman published a highly moralised version of seven books in 1598. He completed the first half in 1608 and then did the second half in 1611 when he reported that his idea of the original changed. He retranslated the first two books as a consequence, making them much more passionate, moving away from his earlier ethical bias in which he tried to see the heroes as models of exemplary behaviour to an appreciation of the '**pathetical**' character of the poem. Pope produced a highly polished version that, while sometimes toning down the darker aspects of the poem, is nevertheless passionate, rapidly moving and noble throughout. He appended notes in the form of a book by book commentary; these comment on the artistry of the poems in the light of previous Renaissance and seventeenth-century criticism. A notable modern reworking of the Homeric tradition is the long verse narrative *Omeros* by the Caribbean writer Derek Walcott, published in 1992 (Faber).

FURTHER READING

George Chapman, *Chapman's Homer*, edited by Allardyce Nicoll, 2 vols., Volume One, *The Iliad*, Routledge & Kegan Paul, 1962: reissued 1998

The standard edition now available in paperback

H.A. Mason, *To Homer Through Pope: An Introduction to Pope's Translation*, Chatto & Windus, 1972

The most thought-provoking introduction to Pope's version

Alexander Pope, *Translations of Homer: The Iliad*, edited by Maynard Mack (Volumes VII and VIII *The Twickenham Edition of the Poems of Alexander Pope*, general editor, John Butt, Methuen, & Yale University Press, 1967

The standard scholarly edition with extensive introductory material and Pope's own notes printed below the text of the translation

Alexander Pope: The Iliad of Homer, edited by Steven Shankman, Penguin, 1996

A paperback edition which includes Pope's notes appended to each book

Robin Sowerby, 'Chapman's Discovery of Homer', *Translation and Literature*, 1

Charts the evolution of Chapman's translation of the *Iliad* as described above

George Steiner, ed., *Homer in English*, Penguin Books, 1996

An excellent wide-ranging anthology of translations and adaptations of Homer from Chaucer to the present

R.H. Super, ed., *Matthew Arnold on the Classical Tradition*, University of Michigan Press, 1960

Contains his lectures 'On Translating Homer'

LANDMARKS IN THE HISTORY OF HOMERIC INTERPRETATION & CRITICISM

In the long period of Homeric reception there are three epoch-making moments springing from the *Prolegomena ad Homerum* of Friedrich Wolf (1795), written in Latin, from the archaeological discoveries of Heinrich

Schliemann made in the 1870s and the theories of Milman Parry concerning the oral composition of the poems in the early 1930s. Their contribution is briefly described in Background.

Wolf formulated 'The Homeric Question' with a clarity that forced it to general attention. The attempt to answer it generated a vast and daunting literature on the subject over the next 150 years. Although no satisfactory answer has been given or is ever likely to be given, it will not go away and continues to haunt Homeric studies.

If we look back now on the arguments of the analysts, those who use what they regard as discrepancies in the poems to argue for multiple authorship, what may seem striking is their over-rationalistic approach. Often they are expecting the kind of logic in construction and connection that might be appropriate for the classic realism of nineteenth-century novels designed to be read but which is not appropriate for poems designed for dramatic oral recitation. Similarly Shakespearean scholars sometimes make much of discrepancies in his plays that would not, indeed could not, be noticed in a production. Unitarians – those who believe in the essential unity of the poem's authorship in the form in which it has come down to us – have sometimes been able to turn their arguments round by arguing that, far from revealing evidence of multiple authorship, these discrepancies reveal the skill with which the Homeric bard blended material from different sources. Nevertheless, the work of the analysts, particularly when it involves linguistic considerations, cannot be dismissed. In the case of the *Iliad*, they have argued that the poem was once briefer, an 'Achilleid' based more concentratedly upon the hero's anger rather than an 'Iliad' in which it may seem the anger is lost sight of in the many **episodic** diversions. It has also been argued that in Book 16 Achilles seems to show no knowledge of the previous embassy to him in Book 9. Book 10, featuring the night attack, has long been suspected of being a late addition. Surveying the plot of the poem as we have it, unitarians marvel at the artful way in which the climax is retarded and postponed, while analysts find a plethora of inconsistencies and the stitching between different versions glaringly obvious. The arguments of the analysts are still of great interest because, where they do not depend absolutely on linguistic considerations, they involve debates about narrative art in which any reader may join, and out of which may come a heightened critical awareness. Moreover, the question of the poem's composition cannot be simply put to one side. Our sense of what they are cannot be divorced from our sense of what went into their making. And our judgement of the finished product will depend upon this sense.

The **oral** theory of Parry, backed up by the evidence of the observed and recorded practice of orally improvised composition in modern Yugoslavia, and continued by his pupil Albert Lord, goes a long way to explaining the obvious fact of repetition of lines and indeed whole passages containing typical themes such as the arming of the hero or the making of a sacrifice. The singer is not an original genius but more of a skilful mechanic. They stress the degree to which the singer works within and manipulates a traditional inheritance of predetermined **formulae** and in a sense does not or indeed cannot say anything new. This determinism may seem obviously to overstate a case, since reason requires that formulae come from somewhere, but it emphasises the degree to which Homeric composition is shackled by metrical considerations, and further raises difficult questions about the relation of the individual singer to the tradition.

The impasse surrounding the Homeric question has not prevented other researches into the Homeric background. Whether or not Schliemann was right in his conviction that he had found the site of Troy, later archaeology has uncovered physical evidence that suggests that the poems have a firm grounding in the culture of the Bronze and Iron Ages of Greece. Convinced that the poetic fiction overlays a kernel of historical reality, later historians and social anthropologists have sought to use the poems to locate the social customs of early Greek society (sometimes using comparative knowledge of other early social systems) and then used the picture so constructed to illuminate the poems. Since there is little other direct evidence, this is to some extent a circular move, but there is no doubt that to read the poems through such an anthropological perspective is helpful and worthwhile. For instance in *The World of Odysseus* (as relevant to the *Iliad* as to the *Odyssey*), M.I. Finley works on the assumption that the poems, whatever connection they have with the Mycenaean world, emanate from a later and more insecure time, the last stage of a period when Greece was governed by petty kings.

In the last two decades, the study of literature has been increasingly influenced by new waves of theoretical criticism emanating from continental Europe and the United States. So far this has made little impact upon Homeric studies, which may seem surprising given the scholarly attention paid to these foundation texts in the Western tradition. In very general terms it might be said that one aim of much modern theory is to unsettle comfortable notions about 'original genius' (often regarded as a bourgeois illusion), about the relation of an artist's work to his life and about the relation of the artist's life to the times in which s/he lives. But since Wolf's *Prolegomena*, nobody has had any comfortable notions about the authorship of the Homeric poems or their relationship to the culture that produced them. Modern critics have sometimes talked of 'the death of the author'. Homer as an author died two centuries ago. Another aim of modern theorists whose starting point is the limitation of language as a self-referential system is further to undermine the autonomy of the self-directed artist. Since Parry, Homeric scholars have been only too well aware of the limitations imposed on the artist by the traditional language system in which he works.

The great question-mark hanging over these productions has had an inhibiting effect, so that it is not merely that the world of classical scholarship has been slow to catch up with modern thinking, more a case, perhaps, that much modern thinking about literary production and the relation of art to society and of the artist to his inherited linguistic medium has already been anticipated in the mainstream, even if the discussion has not been conducted in the same terminology.

FURTHER READING

Howard Clarke, *Homer's Readers: A Historical Introduction to the Iliad and Odyssey*, University of Delaware Press, 1981

An admirable compilation of responses to the poems with chapters on the early romance tradition, Renaissance criticism (much of it hostile), the allegorising of Homer, the debate between analysts and unitarians, and the contributions of archaeologists, oral theories and anthropologists. This sets out in the clearest terms the various approaches, debates and arguments about the poems

M.I. Finley, *The World of Odysseus*, Penguin Books, Harmondsworth, 1962

An historian's estimate of the social reality implied in the poems

Albert. B. Lord, *The Singer of Tales*, Harvard University Press, 1960

A disciple of Parry, who relates the Homeric poems to the compositions of contemporary Yugoslav oral poets

T.H. Myers, *Homer and his Critics*, edited by Dorothea Gray, Routledge & Kegan Paul, 1958

A general survey, emphasising history and archaeology

Milman Parry, *The Making of Homeric Verse*, edited by Adam Parry, Oxford University Press, 1971

Parry's groundbreaking theory of the oral formulaic character of Homeric verse composition

T.B.L. Webster, *From Mycenae to Homer*, Praeger, New York, 1958

Relates the poems to bronze age Mycenaean culture

WORKS OF GENERAL REFERENCE

Atlas of Ancient and Classical Geography, Everyman's Library, J.M. Dent, London, 1950

Includes a map of the world as it seems to be represented in Homer

A.J.B. Wace & F.H. Stubbings, eds, *A Companion to Homer*, Macmillan, London, 1962

A standard authoritative work introducing many areas of Homeric scholarship

Michael Grant & John Hazel, eds, *Who's Who in Classical Mythology*, Weidenfield & Nicolson, 1979

Simon Hornblower & Antony Spawforth, eds, *The Oxford Classical Dictionary: The Ultimate reference Work on the Classical World*, 3rd edition, Oxford University Press, 1996

E.T. Owens, *The Story of the Iliad*, G. Bell & Sons, London, 1947

A book by book analysis of the plot of the poem

M.R. Scherer, *The Legends of Troy in Art and Literature*, Phaidon Press, London and New York, 1963

Chronology

Many dates are approximate and frequently disputed

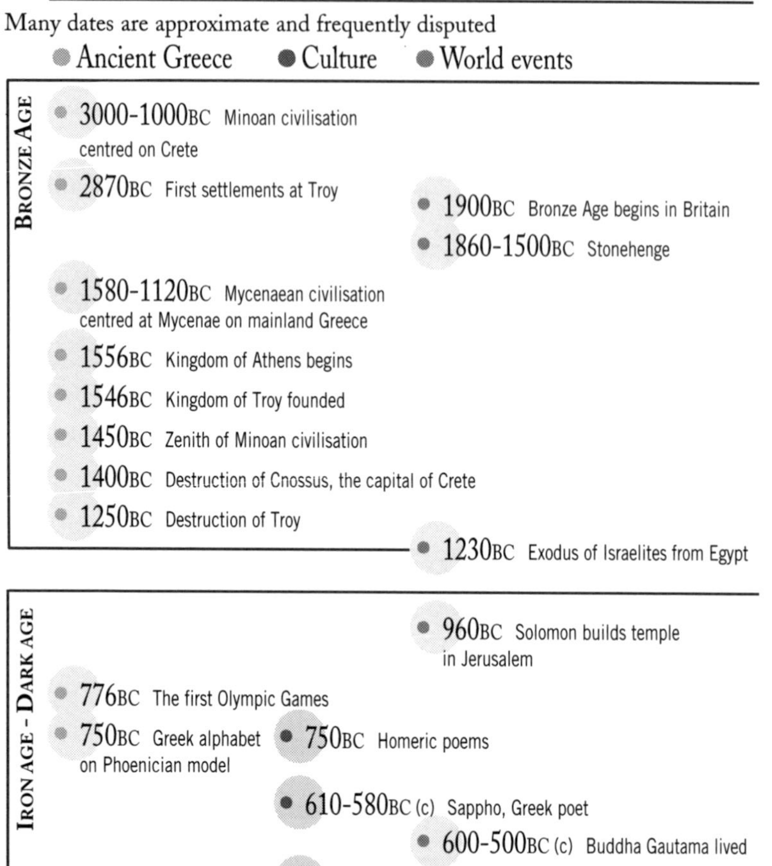

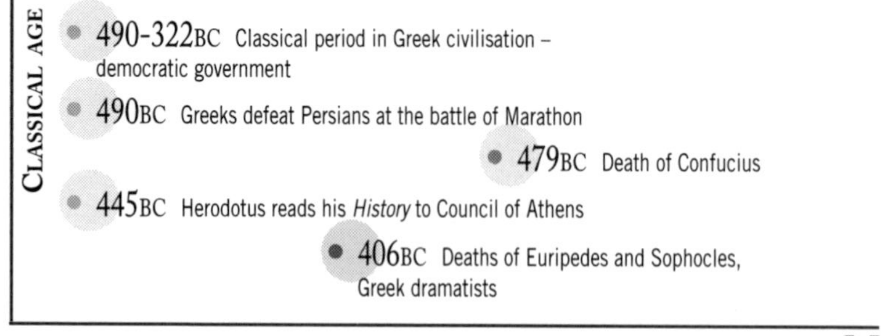

Many dates are approximate and frequently disputed

Ancient Greece · Culture · World events

CLASSICAL AGE

- 400BC Socrates put to death
- 390BC Gauls occupy Rome
- 375BC (c) Plato's Republic
- 350BC (c) Zoilus, sophist and grammarian, severe critic of Homer
- 347BC Death of Plato
- 340BC (c) Aristotle's *Poetics*
- 331BC Foundation of Alexandria on the Nile delta by Alexander the Great
- 323BC Ptolemy I founds dynasty in Egypt
- 322BC Alexander of Macedon completes the conquest of mainland Greece; end of democracy at Athens
- 300BC-100AD Sanskrit epic, *Mahabharata,* of 90,000 stanzas compiled
- 214BC Great Wall of China constructed
- 180BC Aristarchus heads Alexandrian library – Homeric poems edited
- 70-19BC Virgil, Roman poet, author of the *Aeneid*
- 3BC-1AD (c) Birth of Christ
- 1st century AD *On the Sublime,* attributed to Longinus

- 1715-20AD Alexander Pope's translation of the *Iliad*
- 1725-6AD Pope's translation of the *Odyssey*
- 1795AD Friedrich Wolf, *Prolegomena ad Homerum*
- 1870s Heinrich Schliemann excavates Troy and Mycenae
- 1900 Sir Harold Evans excavates Cnossus
- 1930 Milman Parry promulgates his theory of Odyssey's oral composition

allegory in Greek means saying one thing in terms of another and is used rather loosely in connection with Homer. Athene, the goddess of wisdom, might be regarded as an allegorical expression of the power of reason

anagnorisis recognition: Aristotle's term for the new awareness brought about by the tragic catastrophe or change of fortune

aristeia a series of exploits, or deeds of bravery, centred on a single hero

catastrophe a change of fortune

dactyl a metrical unit or foot, comprising a long syllable followed by two short syllables (sounding like tum ti ti)

decorum fittingness, appropriateness; as a literary term it can refer to the appropriateness of character to plot, of language to character or of imagery to theme or to any combination of these. It is a key principle of classical art admirably embodied in the Homeric poems. Occasionally some of Homer's similes for example, when Aias is likened to a stubborn ass, have been thought to be beneath the dignity of epic

divine machinery a collective noun for the gods and goddesses, so called from their use as plot devices or mechanisms. Apollo sends the plague at the beginning of the poem. The action turns on the will of Zeus

epic a work of art (usually a poem) on a grand scale, written in a grand style with heroic figures involved in a great enterprise; the *Iliad* is a defining type of the genre with a unified plot diversified by numerous episodes, and such features as divine machinery, set speeches, formal epithets, and extended similes

episode a part of the poem that is self-contained and not absolutely necessary for the main plot, e.g. the Dolon episode

epithet the Greek word for adjective (derived from the Latin); used of the regular adjectives describing persons, places and things, e.g., Poseidon 'the Earth Shaker', 'sandy' Pylos, 'seven-fold' shield

formula recurring units of sense, repeated phrases (see Background, on The Language of Homer)

hamartia error or mistake, the word used by Aristotle to identify the beginning of a tragic action or plot

hexameter from the Greek word for six (hex) and the word for measure (metron); the metre of the Homeric poems and of all later epic poetry in antiquity

irony saying one thing that has another meaning or implication

metaphor from the Greek 'carrying over'; one thing is described as being another, thus 'carrying over' all its associations; Hector tells Achilles that he has a heart of iron, where iron is not literal but metaphorical, carrying all the associations of this hard unyielding metal

oral poem one composed by improvisation for recitation not by means of writing to be read

paradox an apparently self-contradictory statement, yet lying behind the absurdity is a meaning or truth

pathetic fallacy the fallacious attribution of human feeling (pathos) to inanimate nature; related to this is the description of animal behaviour in human terms

pathos, pathetic from the Greek meaning strong emotion often suffering or, in a tragedy, a calamity causing suffering

peripeteia Aristotle's term for an ironic reversal of fortune, an unforeseen turn in the plot

periphrasis the Greek word for circumlocution, that is talking round a thing rather than directly naming it. A phrase like 'The King of Gods and men' may be regarded as a dignified periphrasis for Zeus

poetic justice a state of affairs when the good are rewarded and the bad punished, so called because it seldom happens in life, only in fiction

rhapsode literally a stitcher of songs; in ancient Greece used to denote the minstrels who performed parts of the Homeric poems, perhaps stitching together songs from various sources

scholia explanatory or interpretative comments written around the text of the poem in manuscript versions of it

simile a comparison, often extended in Homer and a chief source of poetic imagery

spondee a metrical unit or foot comprising two long syllables (sounding like tum tum)

sublime that which is dignified, grand and powerfully emotive

symbol something which represents something else by analogy or association, e.g. a sword representing war

tragedy from the Greek meaning 'goat-song', an unhelpful derivation, referring to the dramatic productions produced at festivals in Athens two centuries after Homer and analysed by Aristotle in his *Poetics* of *c.*340BC. For Aristotle, the best sort of tragedy involves a fall from greatness resulting from an error leading to a catastrophe or change of fortune involving a recognition or new awareness

trochee a metrical unit or foot comprising a long syllable followed by a short syllable (sounding like tum ti)

unity of action a series of actions linked by a probable or necessary chain of cause and effect, as in the main plot of the *Iliad* involving the anger of Achilles

unities of action, time and place. The *Iliad* has all three unities; it has unity of action and unity of place and time, for all the action takes place in Troy within a concentrated period of some forty days

AUTHOR OF THIS NOTE

Robin Sowerby was educated at St Catharine's College, Cambridge, where he read Classics and English. He now lectures in the Department of English Studies at Stirling University. He is also the author of York Notes on *The Odyssey*, Virgil's *Aeneid* and Plato's *Republic* and Advanced Notes on *The Odyssey*, Shakespeare's *Antony and Cleopatra*, *As You Like It* and *Alexander Pope: The Rape of the Lock and Other Poems*. He has edited selections from Dryden and Pope and is the author of *The Classical Legacy in Renaissance Poetry*, Longman, 1994 and *The Greeks: An Introduction to their Culture*, Routledge, 1995.